# UNDERSTANDING DUPLICATE

*with a hilarious look at
bridge clubs and players*

## John Gullick

Wimbledon Bridge Enterprises

First Published 1990 by
Wimbledon Bridge Enterprises
© John Gullick

Printed & bound by
Cox & Wyman Ltd, Reading, Berks

# CONTENTS

Introduction – Disclaimer    5
1. Club Life    7
2. Making a start    13
3. Playing the Game of Duplicate    22
4. Pete Perfidy and the rules    37
5. Conventionally speaking    47
6. At the Ashen Faces    50
7. Think and make progress    57
8. As luck would have it    65
9. Other Conventions    67
10. Other Games    74
11. Finale: a hand from the simultaneous pairs    81
Information    93

*If you have already begun duplicate, skip Chapter 2.*

*If you have a little experience, most of Chapter 3 will be familiar to you.*

*If you are a very serious player, if you don't think that bridge should, above all, be fun, this book is not for you. Give it to a friend.*

# Introduction — Disclaimer

Bridge is played for pleasure. Duplicate too. You may take it seriously but it is primarily an entertainment. So in this book I have attempted not only to smooth the passage between rubber and duplicate but also to entertain; to the extent, I hope that those already playing a modest game of duplicate will find it enjoyable and instructive.

To this end I have built a scenario round an imaginary bridge club with imaginary members. This presented problems.

The first was the name of the club. Giving it no particular thought I jotted down The Elms, The Laurels and The Oaks, only to find that such clubs already existed. So I abandoned trees and began thinking of places. This was no easier. Towns, of course, have already given their names to bridge clubs, Inventing villages proved extraordinary difficult. Who is to say that in the whole world there is not a Middle Crashing or a Bumpingville? A flight of fancy led me to the Lalapalooza Bridge Club. There is one, a friend told me, in the United States.

Then one night a name came to me in a dream. The only way to capture a dream is to half awaken and jot it down. In the morning I discovered that the club was to be called The Ashen Faces.

I do not know why. The club is a friendly one, and the faces are cheerful rather than strained, at least before the game begins. I believe that in my dream I must have seen the face of Herr Unter Bidde when Mr Flutter propelled him into a grand slam, and that of Mr Flutter when Herr Unter Bidde needlessly went one down.

As you see, the players have names too, and in some cases

idiosyncracies. They make mistakes, occasionally dreadful mistakes, they employ the wrong tactics, as will become clear in these pages. This presented a still greater difficulty. I am a member of two bridge clubs and my fellow members are sure to try to discern themselves in this book, thereafter cutting me dead or calling their lawyers.

They would be wrong. I first played bridge long ago, and my memories of the players then and through the years are as vivid as of those I meet nowadays. So I disclaim that the characters are based on any living persons, or on any of the departed, for that matter.

Truly. I have never met Miss Narrow, Miss Joy Pretty, Miss Call or any of the others. If there is a Cambodian bridge player called Pot Luc I do not know him. Nor Alec Smart. No-one of this name has crossed my path. Of course most of us know someone like Alec Smart, but this is not the one you are thinking of. My prototype lived in America in the 1860's and anyway he spelled his first name Alick.

# 1. Club Life

Duplicate can be played at home with eight or more people, but it takes place much more commonly in bridge clubs.

I know that the thought of venturing, an outsider, into a strange building filled with tyrannical, argumentative bridge experts is what most frightens players off duplicate. But clubs are not like that. They are a collection of people with a common interest who are friendly, very friendly or, at the worst, friendlyish.

You will not meet dragons. People are the same everywhere, in your town, in the next town or the one over the hill. Or at the club. You will be made welcome.

I assure you, there is nothing alarming about bridge clubs.

They may be of any size. They may play once or twice a week, or all day, morning, afternoon and evening. They may be contained in sumptuous premises or leaky village halls. Some will have a bar and restaurant, others run to a cup of tea or coffee at a predetermined time.

For the purposes of this book your club is The Ashen Faces. It is in a country town some distance from London, has about eighty members and meets twice weekly in the church hall. The chairs are only moderately comfortable, some of the tables rickety; they have to be put up and taken down for each session because other groups share the room, which is clean but has little else to commend it. The walls are dark green, the floor of unpolished wood, and if it looks as if the youth club has just left, it has.

But the premises do not matter much. The members do. Their standard of play is about average, maybe a little below. some are good, some middling, some fair to moderate and a few less than that. Here is an introduction to some of them:

Mrs Straight and Miss Narrow who play (figuratively) down the middle of the road.
An Tic, a wily Oriental, and his wife Fran.
Major Grieving, who is unlucky, and Edna Grieving.
Dr and Mrs Good, the club champions.
Cllr Beholden.
Miss Judge and Miss Call, who do not always see eye to eye.
Pot Luc and Mr Flutter.
Mr Alec Smart.
Mr Meek.
Herr Unter Bidde, who prefers to play in a part score.
The Professor.
Mr and Mrs Montescue-Smythe, from The Manor House.
Joe and Sybil Brown.
Alice Strong.
And others of varying ability.

As you see we are a cosmopolitan lot. Our flavouring of members from overseas is pleasing but not surprising, for ours is an area of beauty and our country cottages attract many escaping from the rush of city life. Pot Luc came first, then his cousin An Tic, then a business associate, Herr Unter Bidde. Alice Strong, from Tucson, Arizona, is staying with friends for a month. We are pleased to have them. Young or old, it makes no difference. Nor does class distinction play a part. Perhaps the baron and the baker would be unlikely to meet socially at rubber bridge but they will be here at clubs like The Ashen Faces on equal terms. Were a vagrant to appear with a brilliant talent he would be accepted, perhaps after donning a clean shirt.

You can find a bridge club by asking around, through the telephone directory or the public library, or by contacting the governing body of bridge, of which more later. Generally, unless you are prepared to travel distances, there will not be a wide choice. You will have to take what is on offer.

Most clubs require you to be a member, although you can go along as a visitor in the first instance. There may be a small annual subscription, and you will pay 'table money' each time you play. The amount will be remarkably modest when considered as an afternoon or evening's entertainment.

A few clubs are businesses and charge more. The great majority rely on volunteers; a voluntary committee, chairman, secretary and treasurer, volunteers who make the tea, put out the stationery and clear up afterwards. There is no need of money except for sufficient to cover day to day expenses.

Of all those running the club by far the most important to you is the Director, who controls the game, pronounces on the rules and quite often – because volunteers are in short supply – makes the tea or coffee as well. He or she is the umpire, a temporary dictator whose decisions cannot be challenged except by a procedure so wearisome that you won't need to know about it now, if ever.

But not an ogre. Do not anticipate a clone of Attila the Hun or Lucrezia Borgia. The Director is more like a benevolent monarch whose purpose is to ensure that the kingdom is ruled equitably, and that the subjects are happy, or at least content.

This last is the difficult part. For all human nature is here, from the merry to the morose, the excitable to the phlegmatic, the sunny optimists to the despairing and, let's face it, from the placid to the contentious.

Goethe wrote that behaviour is a mirror in which everyone shows his image. This is particularly true of duplicate, which can be mentally testing as well as an entertainment. Success at it is a will 'o the wisp, at times within reach, at others far, far away. The mirror in your bathroom reflects a simple image, the one in the club looks into a cauldron of emotions, some on the

9

surface, some boiling inside, emotions of simple pleasure or irritation to, at the extremes, exhilaration or hopelessness.

It is the competition that makes it so. Another poet wrote that it mattered not that you won or lost, but how you played the game, an admirable moral sentiment, but try it on the players on the centre court at Wimbledon, or on a duplicate pair, one of whom has gone down through forgetting to draw trumps.

Sure we enjoy the game, we also enjoy doing well. Most of our behaviour is impeccable, but there are a few . . . I hasten to say that nobody will dispute with **you**. It is partners who may differ with each other. Many bridge players are convinced that if anything goes wrong it is the fault of the partner, and some will say so, though usually in a pained rather than a pugnacious manner. If it were not their partner's fault it was bad luck – Major Grieving's bridge-playing life is dogged with misfortune, he says – or, if the blame just *might* be attached to them, some sort of Act of God. Alec Smart alas! is one who cavils. On the other hand some players, like Miss Judge, freely admit their mistakes, even when they haven't made any. Thus disarmed, her partner has no reason to remonstrate. Besides Miss Judge is elderly and rather sweet.

I do not want to make too much of this. The Ashen Faces is a pleasant place, in which geniality and good manners prevail.

And any differences we may have relate only to bridge, in the club at least. Away from it Miss Call, for instance, is a fierce conservationist, apparently wishing to preserve for posterity any object in the town that cannot answer back. Her current campaign surrounds a rather smelly Victorian building off the High Street, which Pot Luc wants to pull down and replace with an antiques emporium. She can scarcely bear to breathe the same air that he does, she has been heard to say, but of course she has to at The Ashen Faces, if guardedly. Another of our members is Councillor Beholden, a member of the town planning committee who will have some say in the matter. He is a Liberal which to Major Grieving is the same as being a Marxist-Leninist. But such differences are never aired in the club. They are taboo, like race and religion, though not marital misbehaviour. The discussions we hold are on more vital matters such as what on earth we were doing in three no trumps when four spades was the obvious contract.

Ensuring the contentment of the members is only one of the Director's problems. Besides administering the almost incomprehensible rules of bridge he has to sort out all the odd little things that need sorting out. Bridge players do strange things. They may go to the wrong table, or write down the wrong score. Some are too slow and need hastening. Some are too noisy and have to be quietened. Add to these the fact that half the players in the room are dispirited at the result of the last hand, worse still because they know in their hearts that it was their own fault, and you will see that the Director's task is no easy one. He deserves your respect, and sometimes your condolences.

Why duplicate players may act strangely is because they are concentrating so hard on the game that such as moving to the right table is a subsidiary detail. They are thinking.

My word, how they are thinking!

You need to think. After all, if you play bridge for a thousand years you are unlikely to pick up the same cards twice. So each new hand is a new problem. And this is duplicate, not rubber; an extra trick is not a paltry few points above the line but may be a measure of whether you won or lost. Sometimes you may wonder **what** the players are thinking about when, emerging from a trance, they adopt a course of play the opposite to the correct one. But you will do it too, we all do.

The other reason why concentration is so intense is because the stakes are high. Not money, but the passionately desirable Master Points.

To duplicate players Master Points are positively hypnotic, far more valuable than money.

They are handed out to those who do well, the most for winners of a session, some for everyone finishing in the top third of the field. They are collected, treasured, counted at intervals as closely as Midas counted his gold, and gradually totted up to levels which indicate prowess. So many for the first lowly rank of Club Master, then through many grades via County Master, Master, Regional Master, Life Master (and others between) to the godlike rank of World Master.

Thus a record of your status, although rather a rough and ready one because, obviously, the more you play the better chance you have of winning the coveted awards. You may be no better than someone, a rare someone, who does not bother to collect them at all. But such a triviality is quite unconvincing to duplicate players. Some will hunt far and wide, at times clear across the country, for the magical pieces of paper.

Master Points are the end result of your endeavours. Meanwhile there is the game itself. You play in a club to enjoy yourself. That is why everyone is there, to enjoy themselves. You might not think so from the sighs and laments around the room, but it has to be true. Why else would they struggle to the club in any weather, even when nursing colds or lumbago or broken limbs, when they know in their hearts that they will never be stars?

They will want you to enjoy yourself too. In America I am frequently announced to the room as a visitor from England, to applause so hearty that it would really only be justified if I had sailed the Atlantic single-handed. In one panegyric my wife and I were proclaimed the best players in England, a statement so far from the truth as to be ludicrous. In the event we had a disastrous session – bad luck, of course!

In Britain you will be made equally welcome, although in a rather more restrained way. It will not matter if you play poorly, within reason; then your opponents will be happy to do well. If you do well they will be pleased for you. And you will make friends.

Bridge Clubs need hold no terrors for you.

# 2. Making a start

Rubber bridge is a pastime, a social pursuit and a competition. Duplicate puts more accent on the competition. At rubber you may believe you are a better player than your neighbour. At duplicate you will find out.

You may say that in your friendly gathering the competition is unimportant. Really? Do you play to lose? At least a spark of competitiveness exists in all of us. Some may say they play golf for the exercise, but I have never met a player who would not prefer to win. Tennis players would become bored if they engaged only in lengthy warm-ups and never competed in a set.

Competition exists in our daily lives, even if we sometimes wished it didn't. For many, getting to the office or cooking the supper is a competition against time. Gardening is a competition against nature, marriage a competition between the sexes.

And all competition has its rules and practices. In duplicate there are quite a few, but only a handful that matter in making a start. They present no difficulty, and you will know them by the end of this chapter.

You don't play for money, only the glory. There is no rubber, no above and below the line, no part scores carried forward.

The scoring is the same, except that:

| | |
|---|---|
| for a part score bid and made | add 50 |
| for a non-vulnerable game bid and made | add 300 |
| for a vulnerable game bid and made | add 500 |

So: 2S = 60 + 50 = 110

3D with an overtrick 60 + 20 + 50 = 130

3NT non-vulnerable 100 + 300 = 400

4H vulnerable with an overtrick 120 + 30 + 500 = 650

Honours do not count, nor four aces in one hand. Slam bonuses are the same. So are penalties, with two minor differences shown at the end of the chapter.

That is all there is to the scoring.

**The basic differences between rubber and duplicate are these:**
1. **Each hand in duplicate is self-contained, with its own scoring.**
2. **The hands are passed from table to table so that everyone plays the same cards.**

Thus each hand is a separate contest. Every pair is aiming for a better score on it than the other pairs. Finally all the scores are added up to produce a grand result.

The hands are contained in boards, and are accompanied by scoresheets. You may look at the scores after the play of each hand to see how others fared. They reflect your triumphs and your disasters, your skills and your follies and, yes, your luck or lack of it; an unfolding story which can send you home seeing stars on a cloudy night – or swearing never to play duplicate again. Until the next time.

There are three basic forms of duplicate:
Pairs: you keep the same partner throughout
Individuals: you change partners each hand
Teams of Four: you are one of a team.

By far the most usual game is Pairs, and we will stay with this one.

Telephone the club in advance; on some occasions it will be full. Go with a friend if you possibly can. Some clubs will find you a partner, others not.

When you arrive introduce yourselves to the Director. You will be asked to sit at a certain numbered table, or anywhere you please.

Now for some technicalities. They sound forbidding but will quickly become as familiar to you as the National Anthem, the tune anyway.

On the table will be the following paraphernalia:

1. A table number
2. Boards (or wallets) containing the cards – or they may be handed out later.
3. 'Curtain cards', in most clubs, one for each player.
4. Scoresheets.
5. Nameslips
6. Convention cards/personal scorecards. If they are not on the table they will be lying around somewhere.

In detail:

1. The table number. This stays where it is. You will be moving to different numbered tables, and it helps to know where you are going!
2. The boards, containing the cards, usually two or three on each table.

   They look like this:

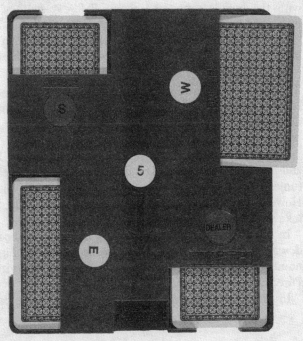

North-South is one partnership, East-West the other. Each player has a slot to contain his cards. The boards are numbered in sequence, show who is dealer, and indicate vulnerability, either with red for vulnerable and green for non-vulnerable, or by the words Vul and Non-Vul. There may be a slot for the scoresheet or it may be kept under North's cards.

At the first table only, the cards are removed, shuffled, dealt and returned to the slots. Anyone can do this.

3. Curtain cards may or may not be in use. They are small printed cards on which the players, again at the first table only, write down their holding in suits, before, during or after the play of the hand. They are then replaced in the slots, face downwards on top of the cards.

After the first round the hands and the curtain cards arrive together, and you must check that they agree. They ought to, but you would be surprised what a muddle some bridge players can make.

4. The scoresheets are known as Travellers, because they travel with the boards round the room. Before play they are numbered by North with the numbers of the boards. Then they remain secret until after the play of a hand when the score is entered, and the result can be compared with other players' results.

5. The name slips. Write your names and pair number in the relevant place under N/S or E/W. Your pair number depends on the type of movement, which the Director will announce before play. There are two alternatives.

In the more frequent Mitchell movements both the N/S and E/W pair numbers will be the same as that of the table (unless the Director announces differently for E/W). In Howells there will be a card in the centre of the table; you take your pair number from the top line.

In Mitchells N/S remain stationary and pass the boards **down** one table after play. E/W move **up** to the next higher numbered table. (Sometimes, just once, up **two** tables if the Director calls 'skip more'.)

In Howells some pairs are stationary. The table cards

direct others to their next positions. The boards go down one table.

The movements were invented by two whist-playing gentlemen in the nineteenth century. They ensure that you do not play the same hands twice, nor meet the same pairs more than once except when the number of contestants is low. No better systems have been thought of since.

6. Convention cards, on which you write the system you are playing (more of this later). Personal scorecards for your own use in recording your results. The two may be combined in one.

All set. The Director signals the start and everyone begins to play. At The Ashen Faces this statement needs some qualification. Mr Flutter is often late, having been detained at his import-export business. So is Miss Joy Pretty, for no reason; in fact they sometimes come in together, which has caused some comment. Two of the ladies have gone to the Ladies, and the Professor is explaining the Second Law of Thermodynamics to Joe Brown, who doesn't understand a word of it. He has difficulty in remembering his pair number. However it settles down a few minutes late.

So then you take your cards from the slot facing you and bid and play as you would in rubber, excepting certain formalities described below. When finished, return your hand to the slot with the curtain card.

North will enter the score, and East or West check it.

Move to another table when the Director calls.

You are allowed fifteen minutes to play two boards. The normal game is of 24 or 26 boards, three hours or so.

Now about North.

This player not only scores but is also responsible for the correct East-West being at the table, for passing the boards down — you may think it curious that when they are due, say, on Table 8 that they should arrive on Table 2, but you haven't played duplicate yet — for ensuring that all the players have thirteen cards, and for pretty well anything else which might go wrong.

You certainly don't want to be saddled with these duties at first, so be sure to sit East-West.

There will be no problem about that, because North-South are usually stationary. However energetic bridge players may be in their daily lives, they become wholly sedentary when playing the game. They appear with backaches, headaches, housemaid's knee or whatever, malaises which make getting up and sitting down positively injurious to their health.

Clubs have two ways of dealing with the rivalry for stationary seats. Either they act on a first come – first served principle; then every pair which can arrives early. Or they demand a toss for seats; everybody who can still arrives early in the belief that possession is nine points of the law. Major Grieving does, glowering away as though to dare a mere civilian to depose a major, although in every other respect he is an old softie. Miss Judge does, sitting there looking pathetic and infirm. Mrs Montescue-Smythe comes with an immobilising pain in her back (Dr Good could testify that exercise would do it good, but of course he can't); she also feels it demeaning to be tramping around the room when such as Joe and Sybil Brown are sitting still. Miss Joy Pretty once turned up with an alleged tennis elbow, but naturally the Director took no notice of that.

Anyway as East-West you lead a carefree life. Just move to another table when asked to, and remember your pair number, which North will need for the traveller.

Now for the formalities – some of them are rules – attached to duplicate.

1. **Before you begin**

   After removing your cards from the slot you should count them face downwards. A careless player occasionally muddles them, with the result that you find yourself with twelve or fourteen cards. The Director can put this right, but not if you have seen them first.

2. **In the play** (the reasons for these do not matter at this stage)
   a) the player making the opening lead tables the card face downwards. It is turned up when partner says 'no questions', but 'carry on', 'OK' or any such remark will do.
   b) In normal practice declarer does not touch dummy's hand except to arrange it to be more visible. Dummy plays the cards on the instructions of the declarer.
   c) the cards are not gathered into tricks as in rubber. You play to your turn by laying your card down in front of you. When all four have been played you turn it over, pointing it towards your partner if the trick is won, towards the opponents if it is lost. At the conclusion of play leave your cards on the table until the tricks won and lost are agreed. They might look like this:

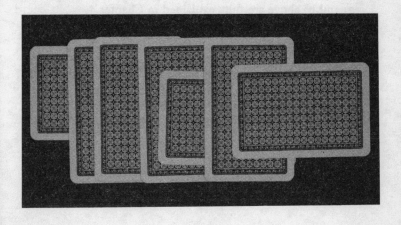

At this stage you have won four tricks and lost three. There is not often a disagreement, but it can happen.

3. **In the bidding**
   a) before opening the bidding at a level higher than one you preface your bid with the word 'stop' or 'skip', i.e. Stop – three clubs. You do the same when raising the bidding by more than one, i.e. (your partner) one club . . . (you) Stop-two hearts.
   b) all conventional calls must be alerted, in Britain by tapping the table, in the US by saying 'alert', elsewhere by one or the other. A conventional bid is one that carries a meaning other than a natural one, for instance a Stayman reply of two clubs to one no trump. It doesn't mean that you hold clubs, so it must be alerted. And get this right. It is the **partner** of the player making the conventional bid who alerts. (You) One no trump (partner) two clubs (you) tap.

   Then an opponent in his turn may inquire of the one who tapped what the bid means, and is answered. If no inquiry is made, no statement is given.
   a) and b) above are fully explained in Chapter 4.

These are the mechanics of duplicate. They are simple and soon become automatic, I promise you. And, whatever you may think at this stage, I promise you too that duplicate is not a game only for experts. You will find that out in the next few chapters.

**Scoring**
In duplicate  50 is added to any part score
              300 for a non-vulnerable game
              500 for a vulnerable game
All other scores are the same as at rubber, excepting these two:

2. Penalties for going
   doubled non-vulnerable

**Rubber**
100 the first trick
200 subsequent tricks

**Duplicate**
100 the first trick
200 2nd and 3rd tricks
300 subsequent tricks

2. For making a contract
   redoubled

**Rubber**
50

**Duplicate**
100

# 3. Playing the Game of Duplicate

Now you will want to know how to hold your own at duplicate.

Of course it helps if you can show skill, perfect judgment, acuity, foresight (every bridge player is strong on hindsight), boldness and caution at the right times, subtlety and flair, and can count on the luck running your way. All the time. But that isn't you or me or anyone who has ever played bridge.

What you aim to achieve, with such of these virtues as you can command, is a **better score** than others playing the same hand.

It may be only a mite better, 110 instead of 100. There may be a colossal gap, 2210 instead of 680. It is all the same, because each hand is a separate contest. In fact your 110, if all the other players scored 100, would be not only the better score but the best one.

You can achieve a better score in many ways, some of them obvious, some requiring fine judgment. The first of the two scores below is better for E/W:

1. By making an extra trick as declarer –

| Contract | By | Tricks | Score | |
|---|---|---|---|---|
| | | | N/S | E/W |
| 3D | E | 10 | | 130 |
| 3D | another E | 9 | | 110 |

2. By playing in a major suit instead of a minor –

| | | | | |
|---|---|---|---|---|
| 3H | E | 9 | | 140 |
| 3D | another E | 9 | | 110 |

3. As defender by getting the opponents down another trick –

| | | | |
|---|---|---|---|
| 3NT | N | 7 | 100 or 200 |
| 3NT | another N | 8 | 50 or100 |

4. As defender by preventing the declarer making extra tricks –

| | | | |
|---|---|---|---|
| 3NT | N | 10 | 630 |
| 3NT | another N | 11 | 660 |

5. By chancing an extra bid and making your contract –

| | | | |
|---|---|---|---|
| 3S | E | 9 | 140 |
| 3H | another N | 9 | 140 |

6. By chancing an extra bid and not making your contract –

| | | | |
|---|---|---|---|
| 3S | E (non-vul) | 8 | 50 |
| 3H | another N | 9 | 140 |
| OR | | | |
| 3S | E (vul) | 8 | 100 |
| 3H | another N | 9 | 140 |
| OR | | | |
| 3S$^x$ ($^x$ = doubled) | E (non-vul) | 8 | 100 |
| 3H | another N | 9 | 140 |

Whether the contract was made or went down, the first line shows the **better score.** Now the opposite happens:

| | | | |
|---|---|---|---|
| 3S | E (vul) | 7 | 200 |
| 3H | another N | 9 | 140 |
| OR | | | |
| 3S$^x$ | E (vul) | 8 | 200 |
| 3H | another N | 9 | 140 |
| OR | | | |
| 2H | E (vul) | 7 | 100 |
| 1NT | another N | 7 | 90 |

Look very carefully at these last three to see how vulnerability affects the result. Always look at the vulnerability before bidding. Quite often 50 or 100 down will show a profit, but –200, no. In a competitive auction for a part score –200 is nearly always down among the dead men.

On the previous page only two results were shown each time. In practice there will be many more. Here is a complete traveller. There were seven tables and neither side was vulnerable.

| Pairs No. | | Contract | By | Lead | Tricks | NORTH-SOUTH | | NS KW Match Points | |
| NS | EW | | | | | PLUS | MINUS | NS | KW |
| --- | --- | --- | --- | --- | --- | --- | --- | --- | --- |
| 1 | 1 | 4H | N | | ✓ | 420 | | 6 | 6 |
| 2 | 2 | 4H | N | | ✓ | 420 | | 6 | 6 |
| 3 | 3 | 4H | N | | ✓ | 420 | | 6 | 6 |
| 4 | 4 | 4H | N | | −1 | | 50 | 0 | 12 |
| 5 | 5 | 4H | N | | ✓ | 590 | | 12 | 0 |
| 6 | 6 | 4H | N | | +1 | 450 | | 10 | 2 |
| 7 | 7 | 2H | N | | +2 | 170 | | 2 | 10 |
| 8 | | | | | | | | | |
| 9 | | | | | | | | | |
| 10 | | | | | | | | | |
| 11 | | | | | | | | | |
| 12 | | | | | | | | | |
| 13 | | | | | | | | | |
| 14 | | | | | | | | | |
| 15 | | | | | | | | | |
| 16 | | | | | | | | | |
| 17 | | | | | | | | | |
| 18 | | | | | | | | | |

SECTION .........    BOARD NO. 1 .........

Note 1. The first two columns are for the pair numbers. The E/W numbers change as the pairs move.

2. Under 'tricks' you may write either the number made, 7, 8, 9 etc, or enter a ✓ for contract made and −1, −2, +1, +2, etc for under and overtricks

3. You do not see the match pointing during play. It is done after the session, probably by the Director. He takes a zero for the bottom score, and then goes up in twos to reach the top; in this case 12 10 8 6 4 2 0. Where scores are equal the match points are divided.

E/W match points are the mirror image of those of N/S. The high score on this board was 12, so if N/S get 12, E/W get 0; N/S 2, E/W 10, N/S 6, E/W 6 etc.

All the match points on every board are finally added up to produce a grand result.

4. Now see the impact of the match pointing on the scores. N5 was doubled, idiotically as it turned out, and scored a top. N6 made one more trick and was second. N4 went down, bottom – giving E/W4 a top which they probably didn't deserve. N7 stopped short of game, for a dreadful result.

This board was straightforward. All the North's played in hearts, all but one reaching game. Vulnerability was of no consequence. Had N/S been vulnerable, the 420s would have been 620s; the 590, 790; the −50, −100, leaving the match points unchanged.


The next hand is quite different.

It was played at The Ashen Faces, where the standard is variable. This accounts partly – but not entirely – for some curious results.

But before you read on I shall first make a sort of confession. On ordinary hands, perhaps the majority of players will be in the same contract, making the same number of tricks in roughly the same way. I think you would be disenchanted with lenghty descriptions of such mundane events, so I am unashamedly accentuating the Alec Smart's, the Pot Luc's and others, to show what can happen – and indeed quite often does.

And because it is more interesting. This follows the old newspaper dictum that dog bites man is not worth a line, but man bites dog rates a double column heading with a picture of the wounded dog.

There were eleven tables. East-West only were vulnerable. The top match point was 20.

25

| Pair No. NS | EW | Contract | By | Lead | Tricks | NORTH-SOUTH PLUS | MINUS | N/S Match Points | E/W Match Points |
|---|---|---|---|---|---|---|---|---|---|
| 1 | 2 | 3S | W | ✓ | | | 140 | 6 | 14 |
| 2 | 3 | 3S | N | ✓ | | | 140 | 6 | 14 |
| 3 | 4 | 3S | W | ✓ | | | 140 | 6 | 14 |
| 4 | 5 | 3S | W | +1 | | | 170 | 2 | 18 |
| 5 | 6 | 3C | N | -1 | | | 50 | 12 | 8 |
| 6 | 7 | 4C× | N | -2 | | | 300 | 0 | 20 |
| 7 | 8 | 2H | S | ✓ | | 110 | | 14 | 6 |
| 8 | 9 | 3D | E | -4 | | 400 | | 20 | 0 |
| 9 | 10 | 3H | E | -2 | | 200 | | 17 | 3 |
| 10 | 11 | 4C | N | -2 | | | 100 | 10 | 10 |
| 11 | 1 | 4S | W | -2 | | 200 | | 17 | 3 |

SECTION ............ BOARD NO. 2

The traveller reveals that the optimum contract for East-West is three spades. North-South are safe to compete up to three clubs, four if not doubled.

In a perfect world all the East-Wests would score 140, but the results are rarely so uniform at any club. At The Ashen Faces the traveller reflects the various skills and temperaments of the contestants. Here is not so much an everyday hand of bridge as a boiling drama.

The first three scores are unremarkable, three spades having been bid and made by West. West 5, Dr Good, also played in three spades, alone managing to manoeuvre an overtrick.

The Director, playing North 5 with Cllr Beholden, competed with three clubs, which was left in. Miss Joy Pretty considered a bid of three spades, and might have made it against another opponent, but she is temporarily in awe of the Director who had occasion to chide her recently for arriving in shorts and a diaphanous T-shirt. We are not prudes at The Ashen Faces, but there are limits.

No real surprise where Miss Judge and Miss Call were North-South 6. On the previous hand they had underbid and missed a game. Miss Judge was not going to let the same thing happen again. Such thinking, if it can be called thinking, is based on totally false premises; one hand has absolutely nothing to do with another. Anyway Miss Judge bid four clubs, which was doubled by the Professor and gained him a top.

The drama continues with North-South 7. South was An Tic,

who has a cherubic, unwrinkled face and is believed to be anywhere between fifty and a hundred years old. He is a wily oriental gentleman – an exact description but one I cannot abbreviate for fear of who knows what – and he put in a wily overcall of two hearts on four to a king-queen, with the intention of foxing his opponents. Next to call, Herr Unter Bidde, was going to bid two spades but was put off by this inscrutable intervention, and rather relieved because it gave him a reason for not raising the bidding. An Tic's partner, Fran Tic, was quite uncomprehending; she passed to await developments. Everybody passed. An Tic, to his surprise – but you wouldn't know it from his smiling inscrutability – made eight tricks.

On the next line you may think it curious that E/W 9 were the only pair to play in diamonds. This droll disaster was achieved by Alec Smart. His diamond bid, he explained later, was clearly one that meant he has three spades, five hearts and a single diamond. Any fool should be able to see that. But such exotic reasoning was far beyond his partner, Mr Meek, who passed with four diamonds to the jack. The result was four down, but it did not end there. Alec Smart is always right and never forgets to tell his partner so, which is why he is known, *sotto voce*, as Smart Alec. Sadly there is a Smart Alec in many clubs. However in his case a dramatic change was to come in his behaviour, which you shall hear about later.

Now to East-West 10, Major and Mrs Grieving, who played in three hearts. A casual observer might think this rather bizarre because An Tic made two hearts playing in the opposite direction. There is a ready answer. Major Grieving held five hearts to the ace-jack. You cannot easily keep the Major down when he has a five card major. The fact that Edna Grieving had bid spades and he had three to the queen caused a flicker of doubt in his mind. It soon went out. A good soldier's duty is to form a sensible plan and carry it out resolutely; besides the major considers himself a superior card player to Edna, who is more partial to tapestry work than to bridge. Naturally he bid three hearts.

| SECTION | | | | | | BOARD NO. 2 | | | |
|---|---|---|---|---|---|---|---|---|---|
| Pair No. NS | EW | Contract | By | Lead | Tricks | NORTH-SOUTH PLUS | NORTH-SOUTH MINUS | NS Match Points | EW Match Points |
| 1 | 2 | 3 S | W | ✓ | | | 140 | 6 | 14 |
| 2 | 3 | 3 S | W | ✓ | | | 140 | 6 | 14 |
| 3 | 4 | 3 S | W | ✓ | | | 140 | 6 | 14 |
| 4 | 5 | 3 S | W | +1 | | | 170 | 2 | 18 |
| 5 | 6 | 3 C | N | -1 | | | 50 | 12 | 8 |
| 6 | 7 | 4C$^x$ | N | -2 | | | 300 | 0 | 20 |
| 7 | 8 | 2 H | S | ✓ | | 110 | | 14 | 6 |
| 8 | 9 | 3 D | E | -4 | | 400 | | 20 | 0 |
| 9 | 10 | 3 H | E | -2 | | 200 | | 17 | 3 |
| 10 | 11 | 4 C | N | -2 | | | 100 | 10 | 10 |
| 11 | 1 | 4 S | W | -2 | | 200 | | 17 | 3 |
| 12 | | | | | | | | | |
| 13 | | | | | | | | | |
| 14 | | | | | | | | | |
| 15 | | | | | | | | | |
| 16 | | | | | | | | | |
| 17 | | | | | | | | | |
| 18 | | | | | | | | | |

He was unlucky, the major said afterwards, to find his partner with a singleton heart.

Which brings us to East-West II, Mr and Mrs Montescue-Smythe, playing against young Joe Brown and his noticeably pregnant wife Sybil.

Bridge is a game which exaggerates the behaviour of the contestants rather more than, say, snakes and ladders or beggar-my-neighbour.

Habits and mannerisms become more pronounced, as Goethe would have added had he played duplicate. You may see Mr Meek nervously polishing his spectacles two or three times during the bidding. Miss Call smooths her cheek when perplexed, which is often. Fran Tic gets flustered, and shows it. Herr Unter Bidde, quiet in everyday conversation, speaks his bids more and more softly as though reluctant to allow them to escape his lips. The Montescue-Smythes can be, to put it bluntly, a tiny bit patronising.

They recently bought The Manor up on the hill, are very rich and much given to charitable causes. They do not speak ill of anyone, nor make untoward comments, they just **look** a little patronising at times, despite the fact that it should be impossible to maintain an air of superiority at bridge when the next hand may show you up as a dolt or a poltroon.

None the less this manner becomes more pronounced when their opponents are Joe and Sybil. Joe is an excellent chap, by trade a milkman. When he bid three spades Mrs Montescue-Smythe was not to be outdone by a fellow who delivers the butter and eggs; actually I don't really know if she thinks like this, the thought may be some sort of sub-conscious one burrowing about in her mind. She bid four clubs, intending that to end the matter. It did. Mind you, on another occasion Sybil would have doubled. This time her mind was distracted by the need for a comfortable cushion and a sudden desire for peaches and cream, Pompadour style. So the Montescue-Smythes ended with not a bad score. Who said bridge was all about skill?

As a matter of fact there is no need to be patronised by the Montescue-Smythes. The members do not know this, but I remember Monty Smith when he was selling lace d'oyleys in the Finchley Road. And since this hand was played I have seen Mrs Montescue-Smythe talking animatedly to Sybil Brown in the High Street, giving her advice I expect. There are some subjects between women which will mellow any atmosphere, and a forthcoming happy event is as important as – nearly as important as – a game of duplicate bridge.

Lastly Pot Luc and Mr Flutter playing East-West I. Mr Flutter is a bit of a one, his current attentions being focused on Miss Joy Pretty, although in the interests of a possible future liaison he does not play bridge with her. He often partners Pot Luc, which is a mistake; they compound each other's overbidding. However they greatly enjoy playing together, never dispute nor complain when they go down one or two, which is quite often. When Pot Luc bid three spades Mr Flutter confidently raised him to four.

The result could have been worse, but not much. Their opponents, Mrs Straight and Miss Narrow, had already extended themselves with a tremulous bid of three clubs. A penalty double would have been quite out of character.

This traveller is not so fanciful as you might imagine. Travellers often show an astonishing variety of final contracts; sometimes because the hands are desperately competitive; sometimes because the sluggards stop in three of a suit when others bid game or even a slam (yes, really!); sometimes an unexpected intervention drives the contract too far or in the

29

| Pairs No. | | Contract | By | Lead | Tricks | NORTH-SOUTH | | N/S Match Points | E/W Match Points |
|---|---|---|---|---|---|---|---|---|---|
| NS | EW | | | | | PLUS | MINUS | | |
| 1 | 2 | 3S | W | ✓ | | | 140 | 6 | 14 |
| 2 | 3 | 3S | W | ✓ | | | 140 | 6 | 14 |
| 3 | 4 | 3S | W | ✓ | | | 140 | 6 | 14 |
| 4 | 5 | 3S | W | +1 | | | 170 | 2 | 18 |
| 5 | 6 | 3C | N | -1 | | | 50 | 12 | 8 |
| 6 | 7 | 4Cˣ | N | -2 | | | 300 | 0 | 20 |
| 7 | 8 | 2H | S | ✓ | | 110 | | 14 | 6 |
| 8 | 9 | 3D | E | -4 | | 400 | | 20 | 0 |
| 9 | 10 | 3H | E | -2 | | 200 | | 17 | 3 |
| 10 | 11 | 4C | N | -2 | | | 100 | 10 | 10 |
| 11 | 1 | 4S | W | -2 | | 200 | | 17 | 3 |
| 12 | | | | | | | | | |
| 13 | | | | | | | | | |
| 14 | | | | | | | | | |
| 15 | | | | | | | | | |
| 16 | | | | | | | | | |
| 17 | | | | | | | | | |
| 18 | | | | | | | | | |

SECTION .......... BOARD NO. 2

wrong direction; sometimes a player appears to have gone insane.

Absorb one lesson from the scores at The Ashen Faces. See how vulnerability affects the results. Pot Luc and Mr Flutter went two down vulnerable and ended nearly bottom. The Montescue-Smyths went two down for a respectable ten match points out of twenty. Always watch the vulnerability when competing.

Earlier you have seen how a good result may be achieved by going down. This is just as true at high levels, for instance when you bid, say, five clubs in the certain knowledge that you cannot make it.

Bridge players call this sacrificing, although I dislike the terminology. If a chicken is sacrificed to an evil spirit, that is a total loss. The chicken loses its life, you lose a chicken dinner, and the evil spirit may not be placated – for all you know it was looking forward to a goat. A sacrifice at bridge is intended to gain. It is a reasoned calculation of how many tricks can be lost to achieve a better result than by allowing the opponents to play in game.

The arithmetic shows what you can afford:

At favourable vulnerability 3 down doubled −500 is better than a score of −620.

At unfavourable vulnerability 1 down doubled −200 is better than a score of −420.

At level vulnerability 2 down doubled −300 is better than a score of −420

or −500 is better than a score of −620.

30

In these cases you must always assume that you will be doubled for penalties. None the less you deliberately go down. This is vastly different from the penalities attracted by the gambling Mr Flutter or the flustered gyrations of Fran Tic. You make a decision based on judgment and arithmetic. And again, as you see, the vulnerability is critical.

Fine, I have convinced you. But now come the drawbacks.

If you were certain that your opponents could make four spades, and certain that you would go no more than three down in five clubs, there would be no problem. But there are no certainties in bridge except that you will get some hands right and some wrong.

Your opponents may not be able to make four spades, then the traveller will look like this:

|  | Contract | By | Tricks | N/S | E/W |
|---|---|---|---|---|---|
| you | 5C$^x$ | E | −3 | 500 | |
| another table | 4S | N | −1 | | 100 |

And are you sure you will go only three down?

|  | Contract | By | Tricks | N/S | E/W |
|---|---|---|---|---|---|
| you | 5C$^x$ | E | −4 | 800 | |
| another table | 4S | N | √ | 620 | |

In bridge parlance these are known as phantom sacrifices, as in the case of the African chief who sacrificed his wife and then accidentally fell into the fire himself. The trick is to know which is which, the phantom or the real one. It is sometimes very, very marginal. Pythagoras got it right in ancient Greece when, after discovering that bit about the square of the hypotenuse, he sacrificed a hundred oxen to the gods. He appears afterwards to have been blessed with a life of unalloyed bliss and popularity, **and** he won a gold medal at the Olympic Games. Actually it was rumoured that the oxen were not real oxen but small wax figures, but the gods seemed not to notice that.

Of course in rubber a high level sacrifice when your opponents are a game up is idiotic. At this moment they are odds on to win the rubber; they still are after you have given away 500 or 700. But at duplicate you are thinking in quite a different way. Your −500 may actually be the better score.

Here is some bidding: You are South, non-vulnerable against vulnerable:

| E | S | W | N |
|-----|-----|-----|-----|
| IH | NB | IS | 2C |
| 3S | NB | 4S | NB |
| NB | ? | | |

Your hand is: xxx x KQxxx Jxxx. Are you going to bid five clubs? Your pair most certainly doesn't have the points – your opponents have. But your feeble collection has acquired merit during the bidding, a fit in your partner's suit, an outside singleton – your partner should have a singleton spade. You don't expect to make five clubs (although you just might!), you judge that you should go no more than three down doubled (although you might!). On balance, in my opinion, you should bid. And may the evil spirit be looking in another direction.

Of course not everyone will agree with me. Not Mrs Straight and Miss Narrow. Not Miss Joy Pretty, whose arithmetic is no great shakes. Not Herr Unter Bidde who would fall into a German faint at the very idea. And Pot Luc doesn't need my advice, he will be in five clubs anyway.

So will other players, for more thoughtful reasons. They will get it wrong sometimes, and so will you. Never mind, there is always the next hand!

None of this is intended as a licence to overbid. It is an encouragement to get in there and compete, the area in which most newcomers to duplicate are deficient. Some seem to think it presumptuous, others are just scared of experienced opponents. There is no need to be, duplicate is only a game. All good players will agree with me about competing. They may not agree with some of my specific examples, but then they often don't agree with each other. If they did they would all end in the same contracts, with the same results. They don't.

The difference between rubber and duplicate bidding can be illustrated in a hand which goes IH NB NB – and in fourth position you hold ten or eleven points. At rubber you might elect to pass; 30 below the line is no big deal.

At duplicate you should bid, a suit, a no trump, a double for takeout according to your style. Opener's partner is obviously very poor, your partner will have some points and a contract may be on for your side. Or perhaps the opener will continue bidding and give away a penalty. This is not simply being optimistic; again it is a judgment which you expect will lead to a better result than if you pass.

Lack of points should not inhibit you from overcalling. After an opening one club, with KJ10xx x K10xx xxx get in early with a spade. This stops a bid of a heart on your left, gives your partner a lead and might even inhibit a three no trump bid by your opponents.

Some stupid bids at rubber are not so stupid at duplicate. A textbook hand such as xxx Axx AJxxx Kx is a dangerous over-call at rubber; if strong diamonds are on your left you may go down heavily. In duplicate pairs the case for bidding two diamonds, or a double for takeout, is much stronger. If it turns out badly, it will for others too.

Be positive. Your partner has bid no trumps and you hold a little doubleton in one suit. If you say to yourself, 'Zounds, I have only a little doubleton, we can't play in no trumps', that is negative. But, 'I have only a little doubleton but I expect my partner can handle the suit', that is positive. Your opponents may not lead it anyway.

Think twice before making a weak takeout to your partner's one no trump on anythng but a very feeble or single-suited hand. With a couple of queens outside a five-card suit your first positive thought should be whether your partner can make eight tricks in no trumps, a better score than two of your suit. In rubber this difference is meaningless, in duplicate it can be critical.

Naturally a good deal depends on who your partner is. It is pretty dangerous stuff if you are playing with Miss Judge, who may misunderstand, or Mr Flutter who will bound on upwards. In practice partners empathise with each other. Disasters still happen, but only sometimes.

So here is another thing. Trust your partner. It is curious how many players trust their opponents to be making sensible bids and begin to doubt those of their partner. If the bidding is wandering upwards and all four players are in it, someone is often fooling around. Trust your partner, even if sometimes you don't. That is the only way to form a happy relationship. Partnership understanding and belief in each other is a cornerstone of duplicate bridge.

Another variation between rubber and duplicate involves the penalty double. I do not mean the obvious ones when Edna Grieving occasionally asserts herself by capping the major's bid, so that together they wander off into the hopeless far yonder. You would double this at any game, tiddliwinks if it were allowed. I mean the occasions when both sides are fighting for the contract. This sort of thing, with both sides vulnerable:

| N   | E   | S   | W   |
|-----|-----|-----|-----|
| 1D  | NB  | 1S  | 2H  |
| 2S  | 3H  | NB  | NB  |
| ?   |     |     |     |

As North you believe your partner could have made two spades. Now your options are: to bid three spades, which may be too many; to allow them to play in three hearts which at one down will give you a score of 100, worse than 110; or to chance a double translating their −100 into −200.

You also have a nasty feeling that at other tables East may not bid three hearts, and North will be allowed to play in two spades.

Naturally what you do will depend on your hand. On the credit side you may chalk up the magic +200, the debit is that the opponent will sometimes make their three hearts doubled. All I ask is that you think about it, not timidly fearful of the consequences, but positively. Negative thinking gets you nowhere in duplicate.

Finally − but there could be much more − here is one more situation for you to contemplate. The commonplace bid of three no trumps. You know that 3NT = 400 or 600, 4H or 4S = 420 or 620, 5C or 5D = 400 or 600. But . . . if you can make ten tricks in hearts or spades, and eleven in clubs or diamonds, can you not make one extra in no trumps? If you can, the result will read: 3NT + 1 = 430 or 630, better than either of the other contracts.

At rubber you would not give a moment's thought to this subtle difference. If your suit is spades you bid four spades frankly and fearlessly. But at duplicate those beguiling extra ten points are a temptation.

Everybody who plays the game knows it. For instance the Professor, a dab hand at calculation, long ago decided that three no trumps (plus one) is the optimum result, and often makes the bid when he shouldn't. There are other aficionados of this score so partisan that they go for it almost as a reflex action. And that is the trouble.

Sensible it often is, especially when your long suit is clubs or diamonds, but other things can happen. Those who stayed in four spades may make an overtrick; your 430 then looks silly against their 450. You may not make the extra trick, even against Miss Joy Pretty. None the less you should not be deterred when the time looks right, even if it means taking a chance. You take more chances at duplicate than you do at rubber.

There is no possible overall advice to be given about competing, except to put an edge on doing it. That way at least you will have more fun. Given a choice, I would rather meet my end as a restless bull than as a lamb led speechlessly to the slaughter.

Either way there is one heartening factor. Everyone holding the same cards as you do will be faced with the same problem. So all you can do is to exercise your judgment as best you can. At duplicate every day is judgment day.

When you get it right your cup of joy overfloweth. When you don't, it doesn't.

# 4. Pete Perfidy
# and the rules

You all know the ritual which precedes a hand of rubber, in which the player on the left of the dealer shuffles and the player on the right cuts. I don't suppose you ever gave a thought as to why you do it. Surely not because you think anyone in your friendly four is cheating?

But then . . .

Somewhere out there, someone you have never met nor are ever likely to meet, is Pete Perfidy whose forbears were famed on the Mississippi paddle steamers and later on the transatlantic run. Pete himself can deal four aces into his hand with charming insouciance. His three card trick is deft and stylish. In his own way he is an artist.

Of course holding four aces at duplicate is nothing special when all your counterparts have the same. But Perfidious Pete is the only one who knows that four kings are sitting worthlessly on his right, waiting to be decapitated. Now that is an advantage.

I have only heard tell of this legend, who must be suffering nowadays from the disappearance of the ocean-going liners; it is difficult to play cards with strangers on a jumbo jet. But it was Pete, Sally Smooth and their cohorts who must have been in the minds of the supreme powers who wrote the rules of duplicate bridge.

By name these are The International Laws of Duplicate Contract Bridge. They are promulgated by the World Bridge Federation and agreed by the Portland Club in London, the European Bridge League and the American Contract Bridge League of Memphis, Tennessee.

Notice that the top brass in England is the Portland Club,

which is to bridge what St Andrews is to golf and Wimbledon to tennis. Where, I think, a member once called for some ham or beef or something between two slices of bread; a flunkey brought it, muttering I know not what under his breath, and thereafter the name of the Earl of Sandwich became renowned in the furthest corners of the earth. But you are unlikely to be invited to the Portland Club, which is on the exclusive side and doesn't play much duplicate anyway. Your dealings will be with the English Bridge Union or the Scottish, Welsh or Northern Ireland bodies, of which more later, or in the United States with the American Contact Bridge League.

Frankly these Laws are heavy going, some of them so involved as to be almost incomprehensible except to the cognoscenti. Nobody in their senses reads right through them, and it would be a losing game anyway because they change at intervals.

Certainly any competitive game needs rules. A tennis player may not have a third serve, a professional golfer cannot play from the ladies' tee, a chess master has only so long to make a move. The trouble is that when a committee begins writing rules it finds it difficult to stop, and then the lawyers are usually brought in to make the language impenetrable. One of the Laws is about what happens if a player bids eight of a suit. It describes the subsequent procedure (and, as a bonus, refers the reader to three other Laws in the book) instead of saying straightforwardly that the player must have lost his marbles or have been drunk at the time.

There is even, despite the Anglo-American special relationship, a clear falling out between the two nations. In England if your partner fails to follow suit, you break a rule if you ask 'having no more, partner'. In the States you may put this question with gay abandon.

If all this sounds a bit daunting, don't worry. The Laws won't really trouble you much. You can go through week after week without hearing anything about them. All you basically need to know is that you cannot in duplicate get away with things which you might (or might not) at rubber.

You call out of turn; you cannot simply make an amiable retraction. You drop a card on the table; you cannot pick it up with a light laugh – it will be an exposed card. You have to leave it there and play it perhaps when you don't want to.

That is the sort of thing. You will not be humiliated or fined or given a spell in the stocks. Any of your infractions of the rules – and we all make slips from time to time – will be accidental; misdemeanours, not felonies, for which you may suffer a pre-scribed penalty, or get away with a mild chiding or even, being newcomers, nothing at all except a friendly comment. It is Perfidious Pete who commits felonies.

Let us return to Pete.

If you remember from Chapter 2, the defender making the opening lead places the card face downwards on the table and only turns it up when partner says 'no questions'. This little byplay is not because the supreme authorities developed a human face, ensuring that the lead comes from the correct hand (although it does, rather usefully). The reason is this. At this stage three of the four players may ask for the bidding to be reviewed. The fourth, the partner of the one who is leading, may inquire only after the card is led face down and cannot be withdrawn. You don't get it? Well, suppose the fourth player were Perfidious Pete, and he were to ask for the bidding before a card was led. He would turn to his right hand opponent and say with obvious meaning, 'Hearts, was it you said? Well, well, hearts', asking Sally Smooth to lead a heart into his ace-queen.

A bit obscure, indeed, but requiring a rule just the same. That is what the rules are for – to ensure that nobody gains an unfair advantage from any call or play, **whether accidental or not.**

Also from Chapter 2 is the requirement to say 'stop' before opening the bidding, or raising your partner by a level more than one. The reasoning behind this is that such a jump bid will take an opponent by surprise; he is entitled to think about it.

Very sensible. Your partner opens one spade. You are about to reply 'stop, three spades' when your right hand opponent intervenes nastily with 'stop, four diamonds'. You need time to decide whether to pass, double or bid four spades. About ten seconds is long enough, and you will probably waste some of them thinking that whatever you do will be wrong.

End of subject? Not quite.

The corollary is that after an ordinary intervention, not a jump, you may not hesitate for an unreasonable time and then pass. If you do, even the dimmest partner will get the message, 'I nearly had a bid, but not quite'.

Here are many difficulties. Perfidious Pete, of course, will hesitate for as long as he dares. You yourself may run out of time because you have a difficult choice of bids. And so on. If the hesitation is too long, partner is honour bound not to bid, in some circumstances; in others not.

Anyway nobody knows what a 'reasonable' time is. Judges have been pondering this word for centuries. The Laws, and the Director's extended Laws – never mind about them – have pages and pages on hesitation, but they help only up to a point. For the record Law 16 proclaims that if a player gives extraneous information by means of a remark, question, a reply to a question, or by unmistakable hesitation – I'm not sure that 'unmistakable' gets us much further – unwonted speed, tone, gesture, movement, mannerism or the like, then partner may not . . . etc, etc.

This is a counsel of perfection. At The Ashen Faces the members do not sit about like stuffed owls. They make gestures, they move, they display mannerisms.

With innocent intent. They are engaged in duplicate, not duplicity.

For instance, Cllr. Beholden is fairly slow at the best of times. A lull in the bidding may occur because Miss Judge is partially deaf in one ear. When the auction peters out at Miss Joy Pretty it is not that she is hesitating; she has forgotten that it is her turn to call. Reminded, she will say, 'Silly me, no bid of course'. It would be a hardhearted Director who then invoked a penalty.

Procrastination is the thief of time. We have several procrastinators. Not knowing what to say next, they will ask their partner to repeat his bid – they heard it perfectly well the first time – which sort of sets the hesitation clock back to zero time. This is a fairly innocent ploy, usually not a ploy at all.

Quite the opposite is Mrs Straight. She fires in her calls like a flash which, I suppose, could lead her to being penalised for unwonted speed. I have never heard of anyone being penalised for unwonted speed, but I imagine it can happen or the World Bridge Federation would not have put it in the laws.

Why Mrs Straight has no need to pause is because she either has the right number of points to bid or she hasn't; she is not often bothered with other considerations. She is equally meticulous away from the club. Assisted by her niece, Miss Narrow, she owns a tea shoppe where the guaranteed home produce is much enjoyed. Indeed Miss Narrow is constantly at the oven, which may account for her fatigue in the evenings. However I am not so sure about Mrs Straight. She would not think of bending the rules of bridge, but I have seen her in another town buying guaranteed home-made food from Marks and Spencer.


Even so, undue hesitation may have a damaging effect on the bidding. Then it is up to your Director to sort it out, often in the face of expostulations and diametrically opposed statements from the two sides. This is indeed a task for a Solomon, which most directors aren't.

Some are very highly skilled. Most at club level can deal with everyday occurrences such as revokes and bids and leads out of turn. To adjudicate on less frequent infringements they carry the Laws around with them, finding themselves being referred giddily from page to page in search of an answer.

I am not really knocking the supreme powers who thought up the Laws. Theirs was, and is, a thankless task. After all, the whole might of the Treasury has proved unable, year after year, to write the rules governing taxation without leaving loopholes for the cunning to exploit. Bridge needs strict laws firstly to ensure justice for everybody, secondly because there may always be a Perfidious Pete lurking in the background. I mentioned in passing the bid of eight of a suit. Why should Pete not bid eight clubs, asking for a club lead?

In the event of an infringement the Director is called to the table. Must be called. It is no insult to anyone to do so. However certain a player is of a rule, only the Director can give an answer, and this may not be challenged.

Well, it can be, by an aggrieved player who wants to take the matter further, to an appeal before a county, the national body, for all I know to the House of Lords. But you won't be bothering about that.

Also from Chap. 2 is the requirement to alert a conventional bid. Simply put, partners must never have a secret understanding. The opponents have a right to know the meaning of any bid which differs from a natural one. If your two diamond overcall means that you hold diamonds, that is natural. If it means that you have a two-suiter in hearts and spades or whatever, it is tapped by your partner, who explains if requested.

This is absolutely fair and proper. But not the end of it. Firstly, the meaning of your conventional overcall should be written on your convention card. This is a printed card with various headings, on which you inscribe your system. For example, **INT** − 12−14, 13−15, 16−18 pts, whichever. **Opening three's** − weak, preemptive. **INT overcall** − 15−18 pts, etc.

Secondly, after the tap your opponent should look at the convention card rather than inquire, although this rule is much more honoured in the breach than the observance. You see, if you ask and then pass it could be inferred that you had something to think about; if you merely pass you could be showing disinterest. It is said that there are certain players in a certain country (that should be wide enough) who, playing against a weak no trump, pass with 0 – 10 points with 11 – 12 ask what no trump you are playing then pass, with 13 – 14, ask then double, with 15 +, just ask.

This is almost Pete Perfidy stuff, and enough of that.

The reason why we do a lot of asking at The Ashen Faces – as at other clubs – is partly laziness and partly because some of our convention cards are not what they ought to be. The Director's, those of Dr Good and others are, of course, immaculate; but the Portland Club would certainly frown on Miss Call, who simply scribbles the word 'Acol' on hers and leaves it at that. Miss Judge has had the same one for twenty years; back then she wrote on it 'Acol with a strong no trump', of which there is no such thing. As result she and Miss Call may get somewhat confused. Miss Joy Pretty often forgets to have a convention card at all. Alec Smart has covered his back and front, with so much detail of so many esoteric conventions as to make the mind reel. He has made Mr Meek copy it too – which is correct, whatever else partners do they should at least be playing the same system – but Mr Meek keeps forgetting. Then he gets a reprimand. Mr Meek remains silent, but lately I have detected a certain something in his demeanour which may mean that he is plotting a grand revenge, such as arguing back at Smart Alec or putting strychnine in his coffee.

A more entertaining offshoot of the alert is when partner taps an overcall, say two diamonds, the overcaller has forgotten that the bid means hearts and spades and is sitting there with a hand stuffed with diamonds. Partner explains that your bid means both majors, which it ought to. Now what?

If it happened to you, you would be dismayed at this turn of events. Perhaps you think it would be fair to tell your opponents. You may not, until later. Difficult it may be, but you should not speak or indicate your mistake by even a start of surprise or a furrowed brow.

You see, although you have misled your opponents you have equally misled your partner, who now confidently bids three hearts. Despairingly (but not showing it) you bid your diamonds again. Partner takes this as some sort of a cue bid, looking for a slam. And so on, on the road to disaster.

Such muddles can occur, particularly when moderate players are essaying a complicated system. Even experts, occasionally. I have seen a pair of internationals finish in six clubs, one holding a singleton ace of trumps and the other a void.

Contained in the Laws are several pages on behaviour, ethics and proprieties. Many are really nothing but common courtesy, such as 'avoiding any remark which might cause embarrassment to another player'. That includes haranguing your partner although, alas!, Smart Alec comes out poorly on this. You may not look intently at another player during the bidding or play nor (obviously) try to see his cards, although it is OK if you see them accidentally. Pete Perfidy will always see your cards accidentally, but even in his absence – hold your hand up.

You may not look to see from which part of the hand a player takes a card; Pete does. And at some stage in the auction Pete will fold up his cards, put them on the table, lean back and close his eyes – a clear indication that the bidding has gone far enough. This is close to cheating although, of course, if Miss Narrow acted in this way it would simply mean that she was exhausted after a long session with the pastry roller.

At The Ashen Faces we are about average on conduct, in so far as any disparate collection of human beings can be average. For instance it is quite improper to show disapproval of partner's call or play. Most of us don't, but we include mercurial characters like Mr Flutter who sometimes cannot conceal his astonishment at some of Pot Luc's goings-on. Mrs Montescue-Smyth's nose may quiver at times. Edna Grieving has been seen to register a look of despair.

Calls between partners should be made evenly, without special emphasis or inflection. However, human nature being what it is, some players vary their intonation. You will hear:

One spade – **two** spades, spoken with finality, or

One spade – two spa.a.ades? with an upward lilt to the voice. The first means, 'I have six points, shut up'. The second, 'I am rather good for my bid'. To be fair, this is nearly always in-advertent.

It could be penalised, but rarely is. The same applies to slow play. No harm is done by being slow when wrestling with a difficult problem, but a player who is consistently slow holds up the whole room.

While we are on ethics and proprieties, do stifle your remarks on a hand until the whole round of two or three boards is over. This is not always easy. Someone at the table may be puzzled or disputatious if the traveller reveals a frightful result for one side; another, delighted at the outcome, would like to savour it all over again. It must be resisted. Once a discussion begins it may go on and on. You will fall behind on the next hand and end up racing through it or holding up all the other tables.

And when you **do** talk, as you are bound to, keep it quiet. If your remarks go *fortissimo* the next table may hear, however unwillingly.

Do not arrive at a table talking about the last hand, no matter how pent up your feelings. For one thing your opponents may not yet have played it, for another it is bad manners.

The fact that some players fail in these departments should not influence you. Be on the side of the angels.

As I said, one thing you must never, never do is to have a private understanding with your partner.

It is absolutely all right to deceive your opponents if you deceive your partner at the same time. So long as partner doesn't know what you are up to you may open a weak no trump with 20 points, for all they care at the World Bridge Federation. You may bid a diamond without any. This is a psychic bid, great fun if it works, no fun at all if your partner, equally deceived, rushes the bidding ever upwards.

An Tic went psychic soon after he began playing with his wife. He did not know then that Fran Tic is not in the least bit wily. She wears a tortoiseshell comb in her blonde hair and three diamond rings on her fingers; none the less she is popular and laughs a lot. But she gets fussed, and on this occasion An

Tic's wiliness backfired. She forced him all the way to five diamonds. He is more cautious now.

Deceive your opponents, yes, mislead them, never. The World Bridge Federation is pretty hot on this, calling it 'grossly improper', despite the fact that Roget's Thesaurus gives deceiving and misleading as alternatives.

Some of Roget's other suggestions for these two words, with my comments are: bluffing – OK; mystifying – OK; bamboozling – possibly; cogging – unknown to me, but better not; swizzling – no; practicing chicanery – certainly not. And the ambiguous hornswoggling, which means both cheating and hoaxing.

Anyway an improper form of misleading is if you hesitate before playing a singleton. Another is when declarer leads a queen towards dummy's ace; with a couple of little ones you may not pause as though you had the king. That is a sinful hornswoggle. However, if declarer has the king-queen and leads the queen towards an ace, causing the right hand opponent to think the king is in partner's hand, this hornswoggle is more of a hoax and OK.

As to which it would be if you set your face in a look of despair when you were perfectly content, we shall have to leave that to the World Bridge Federation to decide.

You see how difficult it is to write the rules.


So the Laws are there of necessity, not to intimidate you. Most of the time they simply do not arise, and will not interfere with your enjoyment.

That is why everyone is there, to enjoy themselves.

Why, up in the highest reaches of the game, when top players battle it out between countries, they are not allowed to speak their bids for fear an intonation carries a meaning; they write them down. Partners are separated by a screen; if they could see each other, perhaps a blink might mean something other than a blink. They are enjoying themselves too, they say.

46

# 5. Conventionally speaking

In the dictionary the word 'convention' is defined as a normal or accepted practice. In duplicate it is exactly the opposite, a bid or play differing from the usual.

Unconventional, so to speak.

You can get along without any conventions, or with those you probably already know, such as Stayman and Blackwood. These are about all you need for rubber. The highest standard (and the highest stake) rubber bridge club in London allows practically no other. This is as it should be. Rubber should go smoothly, uninterrupted by questions about what such and such a bid means.

So should duplicate, in the opinion of many.

Happily most people **do** play naturally, with one or two easy conventions tacked on. At club level anyway. Higher up, well I no longer know which country employs the most conventions. The Americans, certainly, at one time; but now – well, it was the Europeans who invented a system which, in truncated terms, causes a player to open with nothing and pass with a good hand. This one you will never encounter.

Meanwhile if you want to go on calling a spade a spade you will be in good company. But I doubt that you will. Probably you will test the water and find this or that convention useful. And then that or the other. But this is a heady brew. I am not arguing against conventions, at least not much. I am saying that it is totally in error to suppose that the more conventions you play the cleverer you are. They are not, as some seem to think, an Open Sesame or the golden key to Samarkand. First and foremost comes the ability to play bridge sensibly.

One thing is certain. Never introduce a new convention until you and your partner are absolutely certain to remember it. Under the rules you may not refresh your memory by looking at your own convention card. But – and this is why you need not worry about what your opponents are playing – you can look at theirs all you like.

In the meantime – and this is important – it is imperative that you find out from your opponents at the start of a round one or two things which are styles of play and not alertable.

What is the range of their opening no trump? It may be 12 – 14 pts, 16 – 18 pts or any numbers between. It may occasionally be – this usually from the bright young sparks – a mini no trump of 10 – 12 pts. Obviously you must know about this. You may think to compete over 12 pts when to do so over 18 would be suicidal.

Inquire how they play jump overcalls: one diamond – two spades, one spade – three clubs; these may be weak, intermediate or strong. Again this may influence your bid in the next position.

See about their signalling system, probably the usual high to encourage, low to discourage, but it may be something else.

You will have gathered that at duplicate you will meet system bids of one kind or another. Do not be alarmed. They are really only toys, and you know how toys can break. Certainly, in the hands of experienced players like Dr and Mrs Good – they play a few – you may find yourself outmanoeuvred at times, but as club champions they would have the edge on you if they played no conventions at all. Not long ago there was a specially organised match between two teams of internationals one playing all the conventions it wanted to, the other none at all. There was nothing in it at the end.

And anyway the Dr and Mrs Good's may be counterbalanced by tyros having a hopeless go at, for example, the Blue Club (*After all the Italians won everything in the world with the Blue Club for years, so we will do well if we play it*). Really? Do you suppose that copying the cueing action of Steve Davis would make you a snooker champion?

I am not going further into conventions here. Most of those in common use are included in Chapter 9. You can buy a book on them if you are interested. The contents will range from the elementary to the almost unbelievable, and some so lengthy and obscure that they demand a feat of memory far beyond me. And there will be more, not in the book. I sometimes think that every convention has been exhausted – but more still come. As the prophet observed, all the rivers run into the sea, yet the sea is not full.

Do not be alarmed either by the contents of bridge magazines and their plethora of frightfully difficult hands, played by frightfully good players, using frightfully advanced systems. They have little bearing on clubs like The Ashen Faces. Look on them as you would a final at Wimbledon. You can't possibly play tennis like that, but it won't stop you playing tennis.

Many players think that too many conventions are allowed in duplicate. They express their views to the bridge magazines. To be fair there are also rejoinders from the 'anything goes' school of thought. These tend to be from the professionals or the very good players, who have long periods of time in which to think up diabolical ways of fooling the rest of us. They have their right to a say too.

Humpty Dumpty said 'there's glory for you' to a puzzled Alice, and explained that 'glory' meant a knock-down argument, adding, 'when I use a word it means just what I choose it to mean'. Dedicated conventioneers, who open four clubs when they mean four hearts, or one club which can mean practically anything, will applaud this sentiment. For your part, if you continue to bid a diamond and mean a diamond, that is no reflection on your expertise.

Most players do, most of the time. And when they don't – well, Humpty Dumpty had to explain the meaning of his expression to Alice, and so must your opponents.

# 6. At the Ashen Faces

It is not the British way to remember other people's names. A mumbled introduction, and Mr Carew, or was it Crewe or Caruso?, remains anonymous until much further acquaintance.

Of course at The Ashen Faces surnames ought to be known. they appear in the results week after week, but are rarely absorbed. In any case nobody is addressed as Mr Smith, Mr Robinson, Cllr Beholden or Lord Emersley – although at first Miss Joy Pretty called him your lordship until the Director took her quietly aside.

Christian or given names are fairly common knowledge, because many partners address each other in this way. The Director is Jack to everyone. Mrs Straight is Susie – it is Susie's Tea Shoppe, so what else? Some call Dr Good, Jim. There is a certain cachet about using a doctor's first name. It proves that, although he may have life and death in his hands, you are as good as he is. Jim Good doesn't mind. What he regrets is that he didn't join as plain Mr Good, for all the secret complaints he hears of and all the free advice he is expected to give. Joe Brown is Joe, and Mr Flutter, Bert.

But Pot Luc is an 'er . . . good evening'. To address him as Pot would be ridiculous.

There are others like him. Alec Smart until recently did not call Mr Meek anything (except perhaps an idiot) so Mr Meek is also a 'good evening', as is An Tic. And Mrs Montescue-Smythe; it will be some time – a long time – before you address her as Gwendolyn. Herr Unter Bidde's name is Gerhardt, but nobody knows it.

'Good evenings' are safer than names anyway, because of the danger of getting them wrong. Miss Narrow was far from happy when Alec Smart called her a marrow. Miss Joy Pretty's good intentions floundered when she called An Tic Mr Un Toc, the only time that imperturbable face was seen to cloud over – it is apparently close to meaning a dirty pig in some Far Eastern dialect. Nor is over-familiarity popular. Bert Flutter, when he has had one or two, addresses all Scotsmen as Jock, all the Irish as Paddy and the Germans as Adolf. This did not go down well with Herr Unter Bidde.

Duplicate clubs are like this about names. There is simply no time for socialising except between those members who linger after the game, and they are preoccupied less with personal niceties than important matters such as the infernal distribution of trumps on the last hand. I am not saying that the atmosphere is not cordial, or at any rate courteous. It is. Nor should I give the impression that at The Ashen Faces we talk exclusively about bridge. Most of the time, yes, but there are other topics. The ladies have a ready subject in Sybil Brown's forthcoming happy event, especially if it can be turned to reminiscences of there own experiences. They can speculate too on the relationship between Mr Flutter and Miss Joy Pretty who, it was alleged, were seen coming out of The Jolly Butcher together. My word, drinking as well!

Admittedly most of the conversation which is not about bridge is peripheral to it. There are wild differences of opinion, for instance, about the temperature in the room. If Cllr Beholden opens a window, Fran Tic will pointedly fetch her suede jacket, the one with the engravings of the Rolling Stones on the buttons. Mrs Straight, being bolder, will shut it again. The Director will try it half way, and so it goes on.

But this controversy is trivial compared with one which haunts bridge clubs everywhere, around the world probably. Smoking. At one extreme are the radical puffers who think that any restriction on their puffing is a diabolical interference with the liberty of the individual; at the other, those who seemingly almost die at the very sight of the malevolent weed. Their case was strengthened by the discovery, in California probably, of passive smoking. Nobody ever heard of passive smoking until a few years ago, any more than anyone had heard of the environment which, until then, had meant the areas surrounding a town, or a bit of scenery. I am not taking sides, being ignorant of these matters. I do not know the difference between a rain forest and an ordinary forest. My knowledge of ozone is pitiful – it used to be the fresh air which you went to Brighton prom to fill your lungs with; now it is a layer, up there somewhere, or even a sort of poison down here. I do not know the effects of passive smoking, only that as a phrase it is frightfully ungrammatical. Anyway smoking is a matter for your committee, which spends an inordinate amount of time on it. The result is usually a compromise, smoking at some times and not at others. Naturally this satisfies no-one, so the subject rumbles on, and will do so for all eternity.

The members' occupations and finances are for the most part a mystery. Unlike the Americans, who are a dab hand at finding out your business, status and wealth, or lack of it, the British think it impolite to inquire into other people's circumstances. This is proper. In any gathering of a hundred people there will be – this is a scenario, not a poll – 44 housewives, 11 businessmen, an artist, a tax inspector, two shopkeepers, a doctor, three teachers, 15 secretaries, four on the dole, a burglar, 13 factory workers, a computer analyst, a physicist, three-quarters of a peer, a glasscutter and a quarter of a rapist. It is not *de rigueur* to ask questions. The tax inspector might be embarrassed for a reply.

There are exceptions. Dr Good, of course, Joe Brown the milkman, Major Grieving a retired major, Mrs Straight. And Miss Joy Pretty up to a point. She is supposed to be a model, but in reality she prepares the dresses for other models to wear and only models herself if a model is off sick. The Professor is a professor, albeit of some arcane subject which we do not understand.

Pot Luc is known to be in the import-export business, because a brass plate in the High Street bears the legend P. Luc, Import and Export. There is no further clue in his office which is quite bare except for a desk, two chairs and a framed picture of Mrs Pankhurst – hardly a profitable line for export. I once heard a rumour that he imports wild animals for European zoos. If so it is a most unsuitable topic for The Ashen Faces. Major Grieving would recount at length how unlucky he was to miss a tiger when a bearer jogged his arm. Mrs Good is a devout supporter of animal rights, though she has not committed excesses yet.

Bert Flutter is a traveller in toys, which nobody knew until last Christmas when for a jape he brought a clockwork mouse into the club, causing Miss Judge almost to swoon. He is away a good deal, in Aberystwyth for some reason, which is why his mother has changed the name of their cottage from Bide-a-Wee to Coming Holme; as to whether this is an improvement, I am doubtful.

But most of the members are anonymous. An Tic, for all the members know, could be a penniless refugee from some tyranny or a wealthy tycoon. Actually he is both.

How little the members know of each other was illustrated by a recent incident in the club. I was not there, but there was enough talk about it afterwards for the facts to be indisputable.

Just after bidding four spades, which he would have made with an overtrick, Dr Good clutched his chest, paled and fell to the floor. Fortune plays funny tricks in her choice of victim for had it been any other member the doctor would have been at hand to diagnose and administer. As it was, and as you would expect, the members looked at each other with wild surmise. Then Miss Narrow hurried forward, bent down, felt, and called out 'Come here Charlie, and help turn him over. Get an ambulance someone'. Mabel Narrow and Charlie Meek pummelled and pushed and did I know not what to the prostrate body until help arrived and the doctor was taken away.

Then everybody started talking at once. What they had not known was that Miss Narrow, until then considered a mere apprentice bun-making niece of Mrs Straight, was once a fully-trained nurse. Mr Meek – Charlie Meek, fancy that – when not teaching mathematics is the organiser of boy scout camps and has a fair knowledge of first aid. The other members – although much better bridge players of course – proved in a crisis to be of no account whatsoever.

It was also Alec Smart's halt on the road to Damascus. Well, not quite. You will never really stop Smart Alec from going on, but he discovered a new respect for Mr Meek. Now they are Charlie and Alec to each other. This new congeniality has made them a better partnership annd has spread around so that The Ashen Faces is a happier place.

So Fate, up to her fickle tricks again, had, by striking the doctor down, done good all round. Oh!, and yes, the doctor recovered and with Mrs Good is well on the way to winning the club championship again.

If the members do not know much about each other's lives, one thing they do know is how they play bridge. This is valuable knowledge for The Ashen Faces, as most clubs, contains a *pot pourri* of standards and a large number of idiosyncracies.

According to the Laws bids should be made at an even tempo without gesture or expression, and many of our members are at least somewhere near to this ideal; the Director, obviously, and An Tic to whom lack of expression is second nature.

To others this is an impossible demand. They sigh, they mutter, they vary their tempo between unwonted speed and desperate pause. Provided they are your opponents you are allowed to take advantage of these, or any *moue* or grimace or other mannerism. (This isn't cricket, to my mind, but it isn't, it is bridge.) The Laws **do** say that you may draw any such inferences at your own risk; but the risk is small if Miss Joy Pretty prefaces her bid of three spades with several oh! dear's and empty gestures in the air. If the speedy Mrs Straight doubles you without unwonted speed, she will be uncertain. I know that you should not look intently at another player, but you need only a glance at Sybil Brown's face to see the look of despair after young Joe's bid of four clubs; although I think it unkind to take advantage of her, she being in a delicate condition.

You will quickly discover that it is unwise to take liberties against Dr and Mrs Good. That you must never double Herr Unter Bidde for penalties – he will have an extra trick or two in his hand. Conversely, if he doubles you you can pretty well surrender; he will have a holding stuffed with your trumps and outside winners.

The Professor is a splendid strategist, a virtuoso at calculating the odds; his disadvantage is that he is required to have a partner who may not share his ideas. Chances of a double against Miss Judge and Miss Call are good. They tend to compete against each other, the worst partnership bidding in bridge. The calls of Mrs Straight and Miss Narrow reflect precisely what they hold, or a little less. Not for them the tortured dilemmas on whether or what to bid next. They don't.

However Mrs Straight sometimes plays with Major Grieving, when Edna Grieving is away at her tapestry class and Miss Narrow is presumably catching up on the rock cakes; they seem to balance each other rather well. Pot Luc and Mr Flutter are obvious targets for penalty doubles, but not Pot Luc partnering An Tic, as he does at times; they share an oriental chemistry which can lead to some tricky results. You should be wary at all times of doubling the Director, even when he is playing with Miss Joy Pretty.

To double Mrs Montescue-Smythe is of course a form of *lesé majesté*, especially if the doubler is Joe Brown or Miss Narrow. Fear nothing, the ownership of a large house, a chauffeur-driven Daimler, an Aston Martin and a Pomeranian will avail her nothing if the tricks are not there. Pot Luc doubled her at an early meeting, and as a riposte she redoubled with quiet *hauteur*. But Pot Luc and Mr Flutter are sound in defence, and she went down 1000. She took it with such grace as she could muster.

I am not really being unkind about Mrs Montescue-Smythe. You must accept that people behave quite differently at bridge from the way they do in their ordinary lives. Gwendolyn is an admirable woman, with a heart bursting with pity for the less fortunate. She is the local chairman of the Save the Children Fund, and an effective one – it is an awkward child indeed who would refuse to be saved when she is around. She is currently engaged with the Blind Club and makes canapés for their parties, although she would resent being compared with Miss Narrow. She is what she is and cannot help it.

Another example is Alec Smart. Away from The Ashen Faces he is a well-liked and respected research chemist. Although he holds a senior position he would never criticise a junior for researching all wrong. He would patiently explain. He plays tennis, and never reprimands a partner for missing a smash.

It all goes to show what an odd game bridge is.

# 7. Think, and make progress

It is quite possible to enjoy duplicate without trying to improve. Tens of thousands do. They may **hope** to improve but make no serious effort to do so. Good luck to them, and to you too if you are one of them. The game is for enjoyment, whether for social contact, the pleasure of a few hands of cards, or for the sharp edge of competition.

Several polls, asking why people pay duplicate have come up with the same answer: firstly, by a long way, for entertainment, secondly for the competition.

So if you would like to broaden your horizons by joining a duplicate club, be assured that the prime reason why the others are there is to enjoy themselves. I keep saying this, because it is true. Out there in the wide world of bridge you are much more likely to encounter Mr Cheeryble than Mephistopheles, grandma rather than the big bad wolf.

However . . .

It would be absurd to deny that there are not some duplicate players who are bad mannered or superior or irritating, no fun at all to play against. And a few sharp ones, although ranking way below Perfidious Pete. But you meet such people in every walk of life, in sport, in business, in the shops, even when strangers bump into you in the street – most will apologise, some will push roughly by, and a very few will knock you to the ground and mug you.

The merit of duplicate is that you will only meet the awkward pair for two hands, fifteen minutes, before passing on to happier climes. This is much better than at rubber where – if you can find a club which plays it – you can be stuck with Gertie the Gorgon for a whole evening.

Such types ought to be chucked out of the club, and may be if they go over the top. But we won't dwell on them any longer. You will not meet them much, and if you do – there is a delicious delight in doing them down!

If you **would** like to improve – well, this is not a teaching book or it would go on forever. I would just suggest that you refine the skills you already have, because the rewards of skill are much greater at duplicate. You might take lessons at one level higher than your present ability. For goodness sake don't try to learn the expert game in one go, that will only be confusing. Learn to **recognise** hands for what they are and see, gradually, if you can find better ways of handling them.

And remember, all the conventions and bidding systems ever invented are as nothing compared to having a sound game. In fact bidding is the easier part. On many, perhaps the majority of, hands most players will end in the same spot. Even a pair of juggins can bid 1S – 3S – 4S. Yet most players in the early stages of duplicate – and later – concentrate almost entirely on the bidding, forgetting that it takes up only a quarter of the time. The other three-quarters is spent in playing the cards.

This is where the sheep and the goats go their separate ways.

Of course playing the cards in rubber and duplicate is basically the same operation. The difference is that in rubber slight ups and downs are fairly meaningless. So are overtricks. For example, you are in four spades with this hand:

| AJ10x  | xx   | Qxxxx | xx (dummy) |
| KQxxxx | Axx  | xx    | AK         |

You can play this in your sleep by drawing trumps and losing two diamonds and a heart. At lazy, sociable rubber this is what most of us would do. But in duplicate overtricks are golden. You must ask yourself, is there a way of making one?

A club is led and you take the queen with the ace. This is a tiny hornswoggle, leaving the king undisclosed and hoping that the next lead by the defence will be another club, not a heart.

You draw trumps, play a diamond and lose it. Luckily a club

is returned. Play another diamond and lose it. Now you can go to dummy, ruff a diamond in your own hand and, if they break 3-3, throw two hearts away. If they don't break you can still ruff a heart in dummy and make your contract.

To play duplicate well you need to think, to concentrate and to remember.

To remember. But, I can hear you say, I have a bad memory. You haven't, you know. You have a dormant memory, one that is lying around doing nothing. Perhaps your fondest memories will be with you forever, but generally memory is a passive thing which needs to be activated. If I asked you how many lampposts there are in your street you probably wouldn't know. Why should you? But if you counted them and filed the number in your memory, you would remember it an hour later. If you tried.

A bridge hand lasts only a few minutes. If you sit idly, your memory sleeping, you will remember very little. But if you kick your memory to life the difference will be startling, not a hundred per cent – that is for experts – but surprisingly better than you expected.

Of course, before you can remember anything you first have to think it. And thinking is a discipline. You must not only think, but think about the right things. For instance in duplicate it is no use at all, positively deleterious to your game, to brood about the last hand. When people say, 'I can't bear thinking about it' what they mean is that they don't want to but are, otherwise the remark would not have been made. Forget the last hand. Maybe it scored a zero; lamenting it will score a zero minus because it uses up the concentration required for the next one.

And think sensibly.

Miss Judge holds twelve points and is defending against three no trumps. She has won the last trick and is preparing to lead through dummy's K10x in diamonds. The only way to break the contract is for Miss Call to hold ace-queen in the suit. But does she?

Dr Good is defending the same hand. With his twelve points, and roughly 26 between declarer and dummy he knows that his partner can hold no more than a jack, a queen or a king. When dummy went down he filed that thought in his memory.

It is hopeless to try to defeat the contract, he knows. All he can do is to try to keep the overtricks down. Perhaps his partner's honour is the queen of diamonds, in which case the declarer with ace-jack can finesse either way.

The one lead not to make is a diamond. He plays safe and declarer makes 430 against him, 460 against Miss Judge.

Dr Good plays for the possible or the improbable, not for the impossible.

Most players think, at least a little, when declarer. Sadly not nearly so much in defence, the most critical area of bridge. Defenders want to take as many tricks as possible; everyone knows that. They need to give away as few tricks as possible; they know that too, but often it is only a bumbling little thought with no practical application. Defence needs to be worked out, thought about, just as much as declarer play. Is it to be passive, waiting for tricks to come to you, refusing to lead away from an ace-jack in case it gives a trick? Or active? Active is when you see a suit in dummy on which declarer can make discards and you suspect, you guess or you realise that he can make the rest of the tricks. Then forget about your ace-queen and bang out the ace before it is swallowed up.

It is surprising how often players go to bed with an ace. An ace is the dullest companion you can have in bed.


Concentration is not quite the same as thinking. You think broadly about what to do with a hand, you concentrate throughout on doing it. Maybe, if the unexpected happens, you will have to think up a new line. All right, then the concentration begins again.

It is difficult, because the limits of unwavering concentration in most of us varies between a few seconds and a couple of minutes, rarely more. For proof, try concentrating on a single matter and see how long it is before it is pushed from your mind by something else. And concentration is more difficult at bridge because it involves lateral thinking. An expert declarer will concentrate not only on his own hand and dummy but sideways, both sides, so that after a few tricks he knows within a card or two how many of each suit each defender holds.

Such concentration, and counting, is beyond the average player, nor is it necessary to enjoy duplicate. But if you become captivated by the game, this is the way to improve. Once you can count in this way your standard will make a staggering leap upward.

It is not so very difficult if you can work out when it matters. A lot of the time it is quite unnecessary to get a count, nor will you be popular if you sit like a very slow calculating machine, working out pointless sums. The time you take will drive others to distraction.

Because steadfast concentration is so difficult, the trick is to hold it on things that obviously matter, not on everything at once. Otherwise fluffy irrelevancies will creep into your mind.

For instance a two is led against your no trump contract. Very well, that is a four-card suit. Memorise it and start concentrating on the diamonds, the suit that matters; watch the discards, see what you can work out.

Your right hand opponent has bid. There are most of the points against you. The other defender has little in the way of honours, but which are they? You want to know where a certain queen is. Concentrate on trying to find out.

Your hand contains Kxx of a suit and dummy has xx; you must keep your right hand opponent off lead if you can. Concentrate on this, think of ways of doing it.

Of course these examples are incomplete; there will be other factors. I am suggesting that you build up concentration from a modest start, then increase it as far as you can. In a way this is like the old puzzle: think of a number, treble it, take away the number you first thought of. That answer is easy. But, think of a number, treble it, add such and such to it, divide by so much and so on – your concentration and memory will not have held all these moves. Indeed you may forget the number you first thought of!

Thinking, concentration and memory are all intermingled. Let me put them together in an example to show that they do not add up to a fearsomely abstruse combination.

As South you open one spade, vulnerable against non-vulnerable. West bids two hearts, North two spades, East three hearts, and you four spades.

The jack of diamonds is led. This is what you see:

| QJxxx | xx | K10x | 10xx (dummy) |
| AK10xx | J10 | A9x | KQ9 |

Now by stages. Think first. Your possible losers are two hearts, a diamond and two clubs.

Why was a heart not led? Probably because West has a broken suit; that puts a high heart honour in the East hand.

The jack of diamonds? Obviously a singleton or a doubleton, and equally obviously, East has the queen.

For the overcall of two hearts West must hold the club ace.

Memorise: both sides have a high heart, West has the club ace, and East the diamond queen.

Concentrate. If you take the diamond lead in dummy you can later pick up the queen with a finesse through your ace-nine. That leaves two hearts and one or two club losers. Can you avoid losing two clubs?

Play. You remember to take the first trick in dummy. You draw trumps in two rounds. Now for the clubs?

Where is the jack? You don't know. Shall you run the ten from dummy and finesse? That is a fifty-fifty chance. Is there a better one?

Concentrate. West followed twice in spades and has something like this: xx AQxxx J(x) A(J)x(x).

Clear the diamonds and lead a heart. East takes it with the king and returns a club, your king being taken by West's ace. West can now cash another heart trick, then has to give you a ruff and discard, or lead a club into your tenace.

This is an ordinary end play which a good player would see at the beginning of the hand. You can do it too. If you first **think** in order to get a picture. Then **memorise,** in this case three cards only. Then **concentrate** for a final satisfactory result.

Satisfactorily, that is, in most cases. Your chance of the

contract has gone up substantially – but not to a hundred per cent. Dr Good may still get you down.

Go back a bit. When you lead a heart, **West** may take it and lead another to partner's hand. East returns a club, your king goes up and West ducks. Now you cannot avoid losing two clubs to West's AJ.

But most East-West's at the Ashen Faces will not think like that.

Thinking will include perception and analysis. Here is a different, and last example. The bidding goes:

| 1S (you) | 2S (your partner) |
|----------|-------------------|
| 2NT | 3NT |

You had eighteen points scattered about and assessed three no trumps to be a better contract than four spades.

Dummy goes down. What are your thoughts?

Obviously, first, can you make three no trumps? Yes. An overtrick? Yes, and no. Yes, but only by risking going down. Is there anything else to think about? Yes, but not a thought which will occur to rubber bridge players.

What will happen to those who play in four spades?

To your dismay you see that this contract is easy. Your original assessment was wrong.

Only by recognising the situation can you ask the next question, what to do next? My answers will not be very helpful, but that is not the point. The point is to identify a problem. If you do not even know there is one, how can you do anything about it?

In this situation, playing in good company you might assess that most players thought as you did – but you still don't know how many will chance an overtrick. At The Ashen Faces you can fairly assume that the majority will be in four spades. So now, the final question. Will most of them make it, how easy or difficult is it? Or, put another way, can Miss Joy Pretty make it? If the answer to that is 'yes' you must certainly go for the overtrick. Against a score of 420, whether you score 400 or −50 is irrelevant. And you might . . .

These last thoughts are included only to demonstrate the many patterns of duplicate. As you get better, the game gets harder, in a way. Like in golf. A bright young spark will walk up to a twelve-foot putt, give it a cursory glance and hole it. By the time he is playing in the amateur championship he will survey it from this angle and that, confer with his caddie, work out the slopes and burrows, hold his club up vertically in the air, and then perhaps miss it.

This is not an exact parallel because as you improve at duplicate you miss less and less. Instead new and entertaining ways of playing the cards will emerge, your judgment will become sharper, the game will become more deeply satisfying.

There is no end to it. The best players in the world are still learning from bridge.

At first your aim in duplicate should be to score fifty per cent of the total match points, your various ups and downs resulting in an absolute average during a session. The results sheet will tell you if you have.

Further away is sixty per cent, which sounds a lot but is only a few extra tricks, some more correct judgments in the right places, and the luck running your way. Sixty per cent may be close to a winning score. It may even be the winning one.

But not beyond you. There, you see, I have already talked you to the top.

# 8. As luck would have it

Most of the poets who wrote about luck wrote about bad luck. Rudyard Kipling described luck as a besom, an unusual word nowadays meaning a low woman. Bulwer Lytton moaned that if he had been a hatter little boys would have been born without heads. A Scotsman wrote frankly and starkly, 'There' nae luck aboot the house'.

Luck is also the subject of numerous epigrams, most of them false. Better to be lucky than wise is patent nonsense. If it were true you would do better at duplicate on your lucky day than a wise and experienced expert. You won't. 'Lucky at cards, unlucky in love' – or the other way round – is simply irrelevant. Perhaps this was first uttered by a forlorn swain who had just won a packet at rubber bridge, having forgotten his date that night, so that his love made off with someone else.

None the less, despite the skill required to play duplicate well, luck does play a part, although not the leading part as some believe. Major Grieving is desperately unlucky, he says, and tends to say it rather often. But then he is unlucky at everything. A keen gardener, the greenfly swarm all over his roses, ignoring those of his neighbour. His finesses always go wrong. His hollyhocks never saw the summer because of an unlucky packet of seeds. The trumps always break four-one against him.

Don't you believe it.

Of course you can be unlucky. Your opponents may bid and make a slam against you which no other pair reached. You will remember that and maybe recount it to others (who won't be in the least interested). But will you relate how you made an impossible contract because the other side missed an easy ruff?

'Unlucky' players will disagree but . . . luck evens out.

It is true that Romeo and Juliet were dreadfully unlucky, but for every moment that resembles a Shakespearean tragedy there is another which proves that life is just a bowl of cherries. Luck will lead you to some triumphs and some disasters and, as Kipling wrote, you should treat those two impostors just the same. The major is rather partial to Kipling – he may be the last major who can recite Gunga Din through to the end – but these strictures by the master go by him. He is more in tune with Hamlet, who had some sharp words to say about the slings and arrows of outrageous fortune.

The thing is, hardly anyone talks of having **good** luck. They may admit it occasionally, but generally their successes are due to skill and their failures to that mischievous creature, Dame Fortune.

If you want to make friends at The Ashen Faces you will scatter occasional 'bad lucks' to your opponents. It doesn't in the least matter if it is true. It will gain you a reputation as a shrewd judge of the cards and a sympathetic character. Miss Call will be all aglow. Mrs Straight will invite you to her tea shoppe. Mrs Montescue-Smythe will pass the time of day with you in the street.

But be careful of the 'bad lucks' to the better players like Dr Good. He does not delude himself that his failure on the last hand was unlucky; he is aware that he made a mistake (but he doesn't want to hear that from you either!). Nor should you mention luck to the major. It will spur him to remember an even unluckier hand, or to a lengthy monologue on greenfly, or how unlucky he was back in '89 to have walked into a plate glass window, as though it should have got out of the way.

# 9. Other Conventions

I do not know how many conventions there are altogether. Enough, laid end to end, to stretch from St Pauls to Hounslow West or, Bournemouth or Penzance or somewhere. It doesn't matter. Only some come into club duplicate.

First, a reminder that any bid which carries a meaning other than a natural one must be alerted/tapped by the partner of the player who made it. This partner then explains, but only if asked what it means, by the opponent next to bid. This is important. If you are next to bid you may inquire, if you are not you must wait your turn before asking.

You do not tap opening no trump bids, doubles for penalties or takeout, any ordinary responses or any play of the cards.

Failing to tap may lead to the Director being called – **may** – and a possible penalty if the other pair was 'damaged' because of it. Being upset or aggrieved is not enough; it needs to be obvious that, because of the untap, you were, so to speak, thrown into confusion or did something you would not otherwise have done, thereby getting a poor result. Sort of thing. The Director will decide.

Of course you can ask in your turn what any bid means, tapped or not. I had better rephrase that. Technically you have to ask for all the bids up to that point and then put a supplementary question about the specific one. This seems to be in honour of Perfidious Pete, who would put an emphasis on his question so that Sally Smooth would take advantage of it. Nor are most members of clubs very good at this rule. They ask specific questions because they don't know the procedure or can't be bothered.

If asked for an explanation of a bid you are not supposed to say 'natural', 'normal' or 'standard', because these may mean different things to different people. You will have to think of some other reply.

It will happen, often, that in answer to your inquiry the reply is simply the name of a convention, let us say Koch-Werner. Now you may reasonably say 'What is Koch-Werner?' and have it explained. I thoroughly approve of this; you cannot possibly know the ins and outs of all the conventions.

If you think, or suspect, that your partner's bid is conventional and cannot for the life of you remember what it means, you must still tap. Then, if asked, say frankly 'I don't know'. If this makes you feel a silly ass, you are not the only one. It is not uncommon for players to forget their system.

I could go on and on, but it is time to turn to the conventions themselves, beginning with the very easy ones:

Stayman:      after partner's one no trump, two clubs asks for a four-card or more major suit; not having one the opener replies two diamonds. Facing an opening two no trumps, Stayman three clubs asks the same question.

Blackwood:  after a suit is agreed, or agreed by inference, four no trumps asks for aces: 5C = 0 or 4, 5D = 1, 5H = 2, 5S = 3. A following bid of five no trumps asks for kings; replies are the same.

Gerber:       also asks for aces with a bid of four clubs; replies are 4D = 0 and upwards. Gerber is a useful bid directly over no trump openings, because INT − 4NT or 2NT − 4NT are usually played as quantitative.

Now we can divide conventional bids into three categories. The first involves bids which would otherwise be meaningless. For example:

**Bidding the opponents' suit.** You cannot want to play in it so it is a form of takeout, either (1) game-forcing, usually with a two-suiter, or (2) a variable two-suiter, 'Michaels Cue Bid'.

**Extended Stayman:** INT  2C
                              2D − 3D

The responder, having asked via Stayman for a major suit feels no impulse to make diamonds trumps. This bid usually says 'I am five-five in the majors, now bid your three-card major suit'.

**Trial bids:**        1S − 2S
                    3D

Spades have been agreed as trumps. In this case the opener's second bid, 3D, 3C or 3H, is one that says 'I am above minimum, and would like to be in game. My second bid also probably implies weakness in that suit. If you can help there, or have a maximum response, bid 4S. If not 3S.'

In this category also come all cue bids, such as 1S − 3S
                                                    4C

This suggests a slam in spades and identifies a club control.

In a second group come bids whose natural meaning has been replaced by a conventional one through general and constant usage. The easy examples are Stayman and Blackwood. Then there is −

**Fourth suit forcing:** 1S −2C
                        2D − 2H

True, the responder just might have a heart suit. However the bid these days nearly always says, 'I have something in hearts' (for instance Qx). 'Can you add to it so that we can play in no trumps, or shall we go somewhere else?'

**Sputnik doubles:**  1D  1S (overcall) − Double
A profitable double for penalties at the one-level is rare. Responder is saying,, 'I was going to bid, but after the intervention I can't. Partner, make another bid and I may come in'. The Sputnik doubler will hold the other major (in this case hearts) probably a four-card suit which could not be bid at the two level.

Sputnik doubles can be played at the one, two and three levels. For starters the one-level is enough. Above that, at least in ordinary clubs like The Ashen Faces, you will need the double for penalties in order to murder the occasional idiot overcall.

## Five-card majors.

In most countries, but much less in Britain, an opening 1H or 1S promises a five-card suit. Therefore an opening 1C or 1D may be a prepared short suit.

In the third category you lose natural bids which might otherwise be useful. The following are the ones you will meet most frequently. They are in outline only; many have variations or continue with further conventional bids. The first two are frequently used.

## Transfers

Facing an opening INT, 2C remains Stayman, otherwise:

       2D tells opener to bid 2H
       2H    ,,    ,,    ,, 2S
       2S   ,,    ,,    ,, 2NT (or 3C)
       2NT ,,    ,,    ,, 3C (or is natural)

These may be weak takeouts, with the bidding stopping there, or a prelude to game or more. Either way the responder, instead of the opener, becomes dummy. The purpose is to conceal the opening no trump hand, to get the lead into its tenances rather than through them.

The lost bid is a weak takeout into 2D.

## Defences to a weak no trump

As soon as the 12 – 14 pt INT opening became popular, experts began working out ways to counteract its preemptive nuisance. It is easy to overcall with a five-card suit, easy to double for penalties with enough points; but what about the other hands, the ones with 12 – 15 pts and no biddable suit at the two level?

You can have two views on this. Either to pass and hope that the opponents go two down, particularly two down vulnerable, or to find an artificial bid to start your side going.

There are enough choices to make you dizzy – which surely shows how much of a nuisance the weak no trump is – Landy, Ripstra, Sharples, Cansino, Roche, Astro, Aspro and so on. Most are based on artificial overcalls of 2C and 2D, showing different patterns of hand. Partner replies and the bidding continues from there, or dies with the first reply.

This is a matter of swings and roundabouts. You lose 50% of your natural overcalls – 2C and 2D have gone – but you gain a fit in a major suit, if there is one, even a minor suit. You may make a part score of 110 instead of the opponents' 90 for 1NT made, or gain by going 50 down. You may make a game which you would otherwise miss without the conventional bid.

Conversely you will lose if the no trump crashes, or if you go down significantly yourself. In which case it would have been better not to have intervened at all.

### Weak Two's, Benjamised Acol

These are based on the belief that the Acol opening two of a suit, showing eight playing tricks, is a wasteful bid. Therefore it disappears in the first of these conventions, but reappears in a different form in the second.

Weak opening two's are merely hands with a six card major and about 6 – 10 points. They are preemptive, in the same way that opening three's are. All you need is an agreement with your partner as to how you will overcall. One variety might be: double for penalties, 3C for takeout, 2NT showing a strong all-round hand. Or, if you prefer, simply double for takeout.

'Benjie' Acol turns the opening two bids upside down. Two hearts and two spades are weak as above. Two diamonds becomes the immensely strong hand on which you would open two clubs. Two clubs is an Acol Two in an unspecified suit.

There are several advantages. The bid embraces the weak two's and the Acol Two's. It also keeps the bidding lower. An Acol Two demands a negative reply of 2NT, so the contract will be played at the three level, however abysmal the responder's hand. With 'Benjie' the Acol Two becomes two clubs, the negative reply is two diamonds, and the final contract can be two hearts or two spades.

As an overcaller, treat the weak two's as above, the others as you would if they were the normal ones.

Here are three more, not so common: **Baron 2NT** replaces the ordinary reply on 11–12 points with one of 16 points upwards. **Baron 3C** facing a 2NT opening, replaces Stayman, asking for four-card suits to be bid upwards, including diamonds. **Flint** facing a 2NT opening. Responder bids 3D as a transfer to hearts. It allows the hand to be played in 3H or 3S, a weak takeout which is not possible ordinarily after a 2NT opening.

These have follow-up sequences of which some of their practitioners are unaware or can get muddled. This may work to your advantage.

The same may be said of the next one. It is abhorred in the United States and in Britain is the one which draws the most clamour for a ban.

### The Multi-Coloured Two Diamond ('The Multi')

The opening two diamond bid can have one of three meanings, chosen from a number of alternatives – you may see which three have been selected. The commonest, though, is yet again a weak two in major suit.

You may intervene by: bidding a suit; double to show an opening hand; 2NT a strong one. But even if you pass you have a chance to double for takeout on the next round.

Those who experiment with systems light on this one at some stage. The trouble then is the same as with any multi-purpose instrument. Many years ago penknives included an instrument for taking stones out of horses' hooves. I never actually used this gimmick – the horse by then had anyway been mostly replaced by the motor – because I never met a horse with a stone in its hoof. If I had, I am sure I would have whipped out the blade and got to work even if – and this is the point – the stone could have been removed more simply by hand.

The same with the Multi. This beautiful instrument demands to be used, even when a simpler, more natural bid is available.

However in experienced hands it can be a formidable weapon, making life very difficult for you.

You may occasionally meet totally artificial systems, usually beginning with a conventional IC. In a run-of-the mill club few, if any, will be playing such as Precision, the Blue Club, the Modified Blue Club etc. If they do, almost every bid is artificial and taps come in a steady stream. You may, of course inquire each time – if you have the patience to do so.

More recondite systems still, some with foreign names, some unfathomable like the Snake Pass System, will not come your way. Fortunately for us they are confined to special events.

Conventions are funny things. Like other vogues they go in and out of fashion. Once the West End of London was bristling with indoor miniature golf courses. There are none left that I know of. Not long ago, when out walking, you were in peril from dashing young skateboarders. Where are they now? How many still play pinochle or euchre? Or Mah Jong? Where have all the yoyos gone? Bridge is like this too. The Sputnik double arrived as a superbid, gradually seeped away and now is back in fashion. The Multi has been discarded by many who first thought it some kind of miracle. And so on.

Anyway you can be relaxed about conventions. You may meet Transfers, Sputniks, Weak Two's and some sort of overcall of your weak no trump, but they are not difficult to handle.

To relax you further, here is a true story of two expert players using a very complicated system. On and off it began to go wrong, so one of them thought of building in a safeguard. He applied to the authorities for permission to introduce a new conventional bid of 5NT, with the meaning, 'Partner, I have forgotten the system. Please revert to normal bidding!'

This was a joke. But probe it for an underlying meaning, relate it to less arcane sequences, and you will see that there is plenty going for you if you just play your normal game.

# 10. Other Games

**Teams of Four**

Nearly everyone like these, often more than any other form of duplicate. They are less testing and more relaxing, most of the time. The only difficulty is in assembling four players in the same place at the same time.

Two of your team sit North-South. The other two play the same hands as East-West. Later you get together and compare results.

What is different is the scoring, which is in International Match Points, known to all bridge players as Imps.

You begin by scoring ordinarily on a card provided for you. Then, when you meet up with your other pair you compare their scores with yours on the same hands, find the difference, check the table and enter the + or − Imps.

Here is the Imps table. The first column is the difference between the two scores; for example two scores of +420 and −430 = −10 pts = 0 Imps.

|  |  |  |  |  |
|---|---|---|---|---|
|  |  |  |  | 4000 and up = 23 |
| 0 − 10 pts | =0 Imp | 320 − 360 = 8 | 1300 − 1490 = 16 |
| 20 − 40 | =1 | 370 − 420 = 9 | 1500 − 1740 = 17 |
| 50 − 80 | =2 | 430 − 490 = 10 | 1750 − 1990 = 18 |
| 90 − 120 | =3 | 500 − 590 = 11 | 2000 − 2240 = 19 |
| 130 − 160 | =4 | 600 − 740 = 12 | 2250 − 2490 = 20 |
| 170 − 210 | =5 | 750 − 890 = 13 | 2500 − 2990 = 21 |
| 220 − 260 | =6 | 900 − 1090 = 14 | 3000 − 3490 = 22 |
| 270 − 310 | =7 | 1100 − 1290 = 15 | 3500 − 3990 = 23 |
|  |  |  | 4000 and up = 24 |

Here are some examples:

You (North) bid and made 4S          +420

Your other pair (E/W) defended against 4S;
it was made with an overtrick: 4S +1     −450

  Your −30 translates into − 1 Imp.

OR

You (North) bid and made 3NT        +600

Your other pair (E/W) beat the contract
by one trick: 3NT −1             +100

  Two pluses here: add them together
  700 = + 12 Imps.

OR

You (North) saved in $5C^x$ −2        −500

Your other pair (E/W) bid and made 4S   +420

  Not so good, but not disastrous:
  −80 = −2 Imps.

OR

You (N/S) went down in 4S, −1      −100

Your other pair (E/W) made a phantom
sacrifice against the same contract,
failed miserably $5C^x$ −4           −800

  Add the two minuses together for a
  score you would rather forget −14 Imps.

It is very simple. Just add two pluses or two minuses, or sub-
tract one from the other.

There are other ways of scoring teams events, but this is the
one you will meet. It allows for a handy number of Imps if you
do well but also prevents enormous swings on a single hand.
Look, for instance, at a score of 400, equalling 9 imps; then look
at 4000 (unlikely), 24 Imps. If 4000 were a multiple of 400 the
difference would be 90 Imps; if you lost that in one hand you

might as well go home – only you can't. At duplicate you may never stop early without a colossal reason, such as being dead.

There are three kinds of Teams of Four:

**Matches, club, county, or national, two teams playing each other.**

**Multiple Teams** in which East-West move in a pattern called by the Director. The scoring is done at the end of the session, or sometimes halfway through during an interval.

**Swiss Teams,** named after a movement in Switzerland for chess, is the most popular. In this your team plays another team in a match, usually of eight boards. At the end of it East-West return to their table, compare, score all the boards, reaching a total or + or – Imps.

Your captain has another card, on which the total is entered. This total is then translated from a table on the card into Victory Points (VP's of course) and handed in to the Director. The VP's act to lessen swings still further; the most you can win or lose in a match is 20 VP's.

This is still easy, easier to carry out than to explain. And now comes a welcome break of about 15 – 20 minutes. During this time the Director reconciles all the results and arranges the starting points for the next round. The winners of the match are moved to a lower-numbered table, the losers in the other direction. Towards the end the nobs will be occupying the lowest-numbered tables. In the last round the supernobs will be battling it out at Table 1.

Because of the method of scoring, Teams are much closer to rubber bridge than they are to Pairs.

In Pairs an overtrick may have a critical effect on your result. In rubber it doesn't matter, an insignificant 20 or 30 points. Nor does it in Teams – good news for Miss Joy Pretty who rarely makes one – a gain or loss of 1 Imp at the most.

The struggle to play in three no trumps in Pairs, in the hope of making 430 instead of 420, is meaningless in Teams.

Get overtricks if you can, but take no risks in making them.

Your foremost thought in Teams is to bid the game if you sense it, perhaps even stretching to do so. If you don't your score of 170 compared to 620 will lose you 10 Imps. Don't miss the rewarding doubles for penalties. Above all, don't miss the slams. Here are the really big swings.

Teams are more relaxing than Pairs. But don't relax too much. There is a lurking peril, similar to that in rubber bridge.

In Pairs if you go down 1700 (bad luck, of course!) that is only the result of one hand. It is all over. There are 23 others on which to do better.

Minus 1700 in rubber, and you may never get your money back all evening. You need to win two or three rubbers to do so. In Teams that score will haunt you likewise. −1700 is an awful lot of Imps to give away, quite enough to blow a whole eight-board match.

You may even notice that the results of Pairs and Teams are different at The Ashen Faces. It depends on the cards. If there are big hands, Pot Luc and Mr Flutter, who will bid a slam if they get a whiff of it, may shine, whereas the skill of Dr Good in making overtricks will count for less.

If there are a series of marginal possibilities, say three spades, not four spades, is the optimum contract, Mrs Straight and Miss Narrow are to be considered. In extreme circumstances − they have not arisen yet − Herr Unter Bidde might even win.

Swiss Teams are going on all over the place, nearly every weekend somewhere or other. They are open events. All you need is a road map and enough stamina to last out for about

77

seven hours with a break for tea or supper, or at any rate refreshments; as to that you may be lucky, or not.

Swiss Teams are also a prolific source of Master Points. You receive some for each match you win, and a whole stack if you finish high up. And at some events the bounty may be in the form of the hallowed Green Points, sort of superpoints to be spoken of with awe – until you have gained enough to feel blasé about them.

I sometimes wonder why Swiss Teams are so popular. They are really only rubber bridge with an extra competitive edge. You need not know anything much about duplicate to play in them, except for the simple scoring. Yet duplicate players rarely return to rubber, indeed some disdain rubber players as a sort of inferior breed. Yet they revel in Swiss Teams. It is a mystery.

### Swiss Pairs

Scored like pairs, played like teams. Rather complicated and to my mind the most difficult form of bridge. There are not many around.

### Individuals

The merry-go-rounds of duplicate. My description, not echoed by everyone, for Individuals are a joy to some, anathema to others.

They are played and scored in the same way as pairs, with one exciting difference. You change partners every hand.

Exciting, or depressing according to your point of view. Many, usually the better players who have a regular partnership going, understand each other's bidding and hope to win lots of Master Points, are dispirited at the idea of having to play first with Fran Tic, then with Miss Joy Pretty, then with Mr Flutter and so on. And for them to be denied their special conventions – Individuals are best without any – is like being sent out for a walk without any shoes on.

Me, I am a fan. Sure Individuals are a lottery, as much like being on a Big Dipper as a merry-go-round, but they are socially rewarding, a real mix-up, a merriment, given the right spirit.

They are ideal for playing at home, with eight or more people. Clubs play them usually infrequently, perhaps once a month, once a year or never. I think this is a pity. But by now you know that I am no graduate of the school of playing-bridge-only-to-win. I enjoy the varied company of Individuals. I enjoy the fun.

Special movements are needed. Look in the last chapter.

## Novice events

These are limited to players who have earned only a modest number of Master Points. Complicated conventions are barred. Some clubs hold them, and other bodies which advertise dates and locations.

## Simultaneous Pairs

Pairs events played at your club in the ordinary way, but in another way quite extraordinary.

In a typical club event the winners might receive 40 Master Points, the second 30, the third 20, the fourth 10. Maybe more, maybe less. The greater the number of players, the greater the number of Master Points. In Simultaneous Pairs the rewards are in hundreds and thousands, up there in dreamland, with prizes as well, holidays and who knows what.

Naturally your club will fill up. There will be a little more tension, a little extra buzz, extra endeavour. Everyone from experts to duffers will be in there trying.

In Simultaneous Pairs the same hands are played all over your county, across the country, across Europe, and in one case throughout the a whole bridge-playing world. There may be twenty thousand others holding the same cards as you do, and if that isn't a contest, what is?

These hands may be old ones, chosen for their measure of difficulty from events years before. Or they may be dealt by a computer, fairly and squarely, although few of the contestants believe that. They think the hands have been fixed or, if it is true about the computer, that it is either devilishly cunning or has gone mad. You will get quirky distributions, and then suddenly an absolutely flat hand which you view with equal suspicion.

It is possible to play quite sensibly and get everything wrong. At least that is what we say to rationalise our failures. And, to add insult to injury, after play everyone receives a copy of the hands with a jolly commentary by an expert on how they should have been bid and played.

It is all rather difficult − and great fun.

# 11. Finale: a hand from the simultaneous pairs

The simultaneous pairs had ended.. In Paris thousands of results were about to be coordinated.

More members of The Ashen Faces than usual had lingered after play. There was an unusual consensus among them. It was generally agreed that the hands had been set by a maniac, not just your everyday maniac but one who also combined a perverted sense of humour with a total lack of justice. Few were optimistic as to the outcome.

'Preposterous', Major Grieving was saying. 'I had seven diamonds and a slam was obvious, but there five against me on my right, five, mark you. Million to one chance. If you ask me—'. But we know what the major thinks. He has a deep suspicion of any activity that takes place east of Dover.

Herr Unter Bidde commented that he had stopped in five diamonds, which surprised no-one. 'In my opinion—' began Cllr Beholden, but his opinions too are sometimes tedious. To his mind a political plot lies behind every adverse circumstance.

After play they had all been given a copy of the hands with a commentary by a world-famous player. He wrote that six diamonds could have been made on an end play. This infuriated Mr Flutter, one of many who missed it, and Miss Joy Pretty who wouldn't recognise an end play if she were introduced to one in the supermarket. Mr Flutter was doubly incensed because he and Pot Luc had bid two slams that went down and, putting on the brakes for once, had missed one that was there.

This is quite usual in simultaneous pairs. The players look for hidden traps when there aren't any and fall straight in when there are.

The commentator was lukewarm about those who bid one of

the failed slams, sort of disdainful if you read between the lines. Miss Judge and Miss Call had.

'It's easy afterwards', said Miss Call, a comment which drew general approval from the gathering.

Only the professor struck a jarring note. 'It is not a million to one', he said – the professor can be a pedant. 'In any case these hands were computer-dealt, computers are fair, and—'

But nobody wanted to hear this sort of thing. The unfairness of the hands is one of the reasons for doing badly in simultaneous pairs. Bad luck is another one, or partner behaved like an idiot or, in this case, perhaps the French had a hand in it.

The big hands at bridge leave an impression. The ordinary ones are just as important and often more testing. They can sometimes be memorable too, like this one from the simultaneous pairs.

Dealer North. East-West vulnerable.

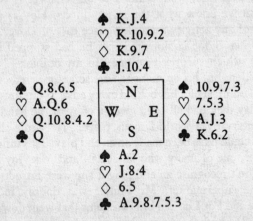

An ordinary collection of cards, you may think, with 20 points each side. But now look closely at what may happen.

North may open a weak no trump – the 10's and 9's make this a not unreasonable bid non-vulnerable. If so, South may reply – I am not talking about experts – two clubs, intending next to bid three clubs as a weak takeout; an immediate three clubs, which is nonsense but the call of such as Miss Judge; pass; two no trumps; or three no trumps. This last would be the professor's choice. He would reason that if everything went well – very well – the contract might make with his six-card suit. He could be right at that.

If North passes, South may pass, open one club or three clubs. West will double one club for takeout or bid a diamond. Depending on what North now does, it is not impossible that East will come in with one spade. Then it is open house.

If the first three players pass, West may open a diamond. Then what?

The commentator, of course, will note that the sensible contract is three clubs by North-South. He is right, dash him, but he did not have to bid this hand in the challenging circumstances of a simultaneous pairs at The Ashen Faces.

As you can guess by now, all sorts of things happened at the club, some of which had never entered the head of this expert.

Some contracts were indeed played in three clubs – honestly, we do have some steady pairs at The Ashen Faces – others in two or three no trumps, with varying success. But we will not bother with these mundane matters.

### Major and Mrs Grieving (N/S)

The Major opened one no trump. Edna Grieving replied with three clubs; this ought to show a hand capable of being played in five clubs if there is a flaw in no trumps. It doesn't. The Major bid three no trumps, with the sort of finality with which he used to dismiss the sergeant-major from his presence. When Edna bid four clubs he crossly raised to five. Two down after a diamond lead.

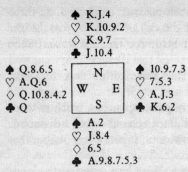

```
              ♠ K.J.4
              ♡ K.10.9.2
              ◇ K.9.7
              ♣ J.10.4
♠ Q.8.6.5       N         ♠ 10.9.7.3
♡ A.Q.6    W       E      ♡ 7.5.3
◇ Q.10.8.4.2    S         ◇ A.J.3
♣ Q                       ♣ K.6.2
              ♠ A.2
              ♡ J.8.4
              ◇ 6.5
              ♣ A.9.8.7.5.3
```

**Pot Luc and Mr Flutter (N/S)**

By now you can be sure that they played in six clubs. After one no trump – two clubs – two hearts – Pot Luc bid four clubs. Mr Flutter knows a slam try when he hears one, even if it isn't. He bid four no trumps. Mr Flutter decided not to fool around. Six clubs was doubled and went three down.

**Alice Strong and Count de Pom (N/S)**

I didn't quite catch the name of Alice's guest, but it sounded like this. As I have said before, we are a tolerant lot at The Ashen Faces, and we can easily absorb a French aristocrat, even one who sounds like an apple.

The French and the Americans play a strong no trump and five-card majors. However Alice Strong, who has been visiting us frequently in the last month, has had some painful experiences. Cllr Beholden and Mr Meek have both passed her strong no trump with ten points. She has been driven to a weak one in self defence.

She forgot she was playing with an apple and opened a misleading no trump.

The reply was two clubs – some sort of holding bid in the European Community, I dare say, Alice tapped Stayman and bid two hearts.

Now the apple took a deep look into the heart of the compiler of the hands. Three no trumps was the obvious bid, so obvious as to be a snare for the unsophisticated. Four hearts, he said with Gallic cunning.

West led a spade.

Alice counted her losers. Two diamonds if the ace was wrong. Two hearts possibly, even two clubs with the sort of luck she had been having. And if the trumps did not break – it was all her fault, she knew, wishing she were back in Tucson, Arizona.

She took the spade with the jack, led back to the ace and played the eight of hearts. It held. Another heart, and West upped with the ace.

West, for his part, saw that the defence was hopeless. Declarer and dummy should have about 25 or 26 points, she had twelve. There was a sort of a wild chance – such as when all the horses but one fall in a steeplechase – that her partner held the ace of clubs, If so, she could get a ruff. She led her singleton queen.

Alice took the trick, drew the last two trumps together, and gave up a club. She lost one heart, one club and one diamond.

In the books I read about the French the characters always seem to say 'Zut, alors' when emotionally moved. 'Zut, alors,' said the count.

## Mrs Straight and Miss Narrow (N/S)

Mrs Straight, of course, did not open on the North hand. Nor did Miss Narrow as South; it is contrary to all her principles to open on nine points or, stretching it, on eleven. After reflection West also passed. A passed hand all round scores 0, which may or may not be a good score.

## Cllr Beholden and Mr Dowting (E/W)

After three passes Mr Dowting opened a diamond. North doubled for takeout. Cllr Beholden went into a committee of one, heard the pro's and con's and decided on one spade. South bid three clubs.

Mr Dowting, living up to his name, now began to doubt everyone, not least his partner. But he has some respect for the councillor, believing him to be some sort of power in the town. He closed his eyes and bid three spades.

Cllr Beholden reconvened the committee. Against another bid: he was not enamoured of his spade suit nor the position of the king of clubs, and he didn't have much of a hand anyway.

In favour of four spades: North's double after passing was plainly weak. South's bid of three clubs was no more than an impudent attempt to interfere with the proper course of

♠ K.J.4
♡ K.10.9.2
◇ K.9.7
♣ J.10.4

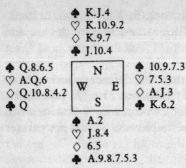

♠ Q.8.6.5     ♠ 10.9.7.3
♡ A.Q.6      ♡ 7.5.3
◇ Q.10.8.4.2  ◇ A.J.3
♣ Q         ♣ K.6.2

♠ A.2
♡ J.8.4
◇ 6.5
♣ A.9.8.7.5.3

events – rather like those ratepayers who kept on complaining. Mr Dowting had opened and had a strong hand. If he, Cllr Beholden, passed the world-famous commentator would probably write, although not in these words, that anyone who stopped short of game was a cowardly jackass.

You can convince yourself of anything if you try hard enough. By a majority vote he bid four spades.

North, whose opinion of the councillor is quite different from that of Mr Dowting – he thinks he is a pompous ass – doubled. Three down.

## Mr and Mrs Montescue-Smythe (E/W)

After three passed Mrs Montescue-Smythe opened a diamond, doubled by North. Mr Montescue-Smythe bid two diamonds, which went peacefully round.

The contract succeeded after North foolishly led a low heart. 'Well played', said North quickly. This is a coded expression, intended to divert partner's attention from a mistake.

Mrs Montescue-Smythe smiled graciously.

## Alec Smart and Mr Meek

It may seem bizarre that **East-West** should play in clubs, but . . .

After three passes Smart Alec opened – it was inevitable – a scientific one club.

North doubled and Charlie Meek bid one no trump. There was nothing South could do but pass.

At this point Smart Alec considered the Scheringot-Kamperove relay bid of two clubs, which of course shows five diamonds and one of the majors, or the other way round, or six hearts and two singletons or something or other. He resisted it.

Nowadays he is on good terms with Charlie, who might forget the response, if there is one. Time to make everything clear. He bid two diamonds.

Yes, it was clear to Charlie. His partner held at least five clubs, four diamonds and a strong hand. With support for both suits he too would make everything clear. He bid four clubs.

I stayed silent as South. What else could I do? Besides it was obvious that Smart Alec would find a better resting place. I was wrong.

Smart Alec was not happy. He knew, of course, that his opening bid of one club was the expert one. Now here was Charlie up to his old muddles again. What next? There appeared to be nowhere at all to go. Then his reasoning took over. His partner had no four-card major (Poor Charlie! he dislikes bidding on four to a ten). Nor did he hold diamonds. He must have a suit of clubs, probably five or six, and some scattered honours. (I told you you can talk yourself into anything.)

'No bid', said Smart Alec. He took four tricks, two diamonds, a heart and a club. Six down.

'Sorry Charlie,' he said.

'Never mind, it wasn't doubled', said Charlie Meek. You see how it is these days.

As for me, I had probably scored a top, if a lucky one. I was wrong about that too.

---

Now for some of the hands played in no trumps. The first is noteworthy because it was the only one played by East-West.

### Joe and Sybil Brown (E/W)

v

### The professor and Herr Unter Bidde (N/S)

The professor's practice on hands like that of North is to wait and see, And it would be quite foreign to Herr Unter Bidde's nature to open as South. Young Joe opened a diamond.

The professor continued to wait and see. Sybil Brown replied

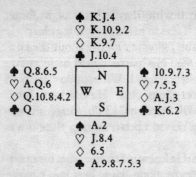

|  | ♠ K.J.4 |  |
|---|---|---|
|  | ♡ K.10.9.2 |  |
|  | ◇ K.9.7 |  |
|  | ♣ J.10.4 |  |
| ♠ Q.8.6.5 |  | ♠ 10.9.7.3 |
| ♡ A.Q.6 | N | ♡ 7.5.3 |
| ◇ Q.10.8.4.2 | W   E | ◇ A.J.3 |
| ♣ Q | S | ♣ K.6.2 |
|  | ♠ A.2 |  |
|  | ♡ J.8.4 |  |
|  | ◇ 6.5 |  |
|  | ♣ A.9.8.7.5.3 |  |

one no trump (they will do these things). The Herr passed, so did Joe. Now the professor was in no doubt. The opposition was weak. He doubled for takeout.

Herr Unter Bidde was in no doubt either. With his two aces and six-card suit he was delighted to hear a penalty double.

He led a club. Sybil Brown took five diamonds, a club and a heart for one no trump doubled.

### Dr and Mrs Good

Just the sort of hand they dislike. After one no trump by North, Dr Good realised that, according to what the computer decided, any one of about five contracts could be the right one. He bid three no trumps, optimistically.

After a spade lead Mrs Good banged out the ace of clubs and another, and East was back on lead again. A heart was led to the ace and now the contract can be easily defeated provided the queen or ten of diamonds is led. A low one was, taken by the jack. A spade came back. Mrs Good reeled off the clubs, and when East discarded two hearts, had no difficulty in taking the heart finesse. Ten tricks.

### Young Sparks 1 and 2 (N/S)

Most visitors when they arrive show some deference to their new surroundings. These two young sparks didn't They responded to 'good evenings' with grunts. They *scattered* things. They carried their detailed convention cards with an air of contemptuous superiority which plainly said that they were going to clean up the old fuddy-duddies at The Ashen Faces. Their appearance was that of apprentice gangsters, though rather more poorly attired. One had a beard on one side of his face only, a repulsive sight although Miss Joy Pretty said it was fashionable. Tolerant we may be, but they will not be allowed in again.

They arrived at An Tic's table, gloating loudly about the last hand. When this showed no sign of abating, 'Next hand', said An Tic.

'Okay poppa', replied one of them.

After two passes Young Spark 1 opened one no trump on the South hand. This is the mini no trump bid on 10 – 12 points, although this time it contained only nine. Young Spark 2 glanced at his opponents. He saw an old Chinaman with an obviously fatuous woman, the sort of easy meat that he delights in grinding under his booted feet. Three no trumps, he replied.

If any young spark had addressed one of An Tic's ancestors as Poppa he would have been subjected to the water torture or death by a thousand cuts. An Tic employed a more civilised revenge. He doubled and led the ten of diamonds. After five diamond tricks he smoothly led the ace of hearts and another.

By now Young Spark I had the appearance of a gangster who had attended an affray, having left his weapons in the wardrobe at home. He put up the king of hearts. An Tic made five diamonds, two hearts and club. Four down doubled.

An Tic, now playing the role of Job's comforter, had one last card to play. 'Bad luck', he said.

## Miss Call and Miss Judge

They were modest afterwards when congratulated on their outstanding result.

Miss Call opened one no trump and Miss Judge replied three clubs. This is standard for her. Miss Call bid three no trumps and Miss Judge four clubs, again predictable.

Miss Call bid four diamonds on the North hand, which needs some explanation. She had at first been a trifle perplexed at the four club bid, until she remembered that they had decided to try out Gerber, and she was being asked for aces. Not having any she bid four diamonds.

Miss Judge was even more perplexed. Her partner had opened a weak no trump and was now bidding like there was no tomorrow. She could only surmise that Miss Call had found another ace or two in her hand, possibly stuck behind another card – and not for the first time either. She bid six no trumps, which was doubled.

The defenders were Miss Joy Pretty and a friend, Maisie Delice.

After a spade lead Miss Call led the jack of clubs. Naturally Miss Joy Pretty covered, so the king and queeen fell together under the ace.

Still there were two missing aces and a frightful danger in diamonds. At trick three Miss Call staked everything by leading the jack of hearts.

Maisie Delice had been unhappy to see her queen of clubs decapitated. She had no intention of wasting the ace of hearts. She put it up.

And returned her partner's spade lead.

Miss Call made six clubs, three spades and three hearts and, was, I should think, the only player in the world who bid and made six no trumps. One up to The Ashen Faces, in a sort of a way.

This was the traveller:

| Contract | By | Tricks | N/S | E/W | Match points N/S | Match points E/W |
|---|---|---|---|---|---|---|
| 5C | Major and Mrs Grieving (N/S) | −2 | | 100 | 7 | 31 |
| 6C[x] | Pot Luc and Mrs Flutter (N/S) | −3 | | 500 | 2 | 36 |
| 4H | Alice Strong and Count de Pom (N/S) | ✓ | 420 | | 30 | 8 |
| | Mrs Straight and Miss Narrow (N/S) | | 0 | | 16 | 22 |
| | Passed out. | | | | | |
| 4S[x] | Cllr Beholden and Mrs Dowting (E/W) | −3 | 800 | | 36 | 2 |
| 2D | Mr & Mrs Montescue-Smythe (E/W) | ✓ | | 90 | 10 | 28 |
| 4C | Alec Smart and Mr Meek (E/W) | −6 | 600 | | 34 | 4 |
| INT[x] | Joe and Sybil Brown (E/W) | ✓ | | 180 | 4 | 34 |
| 3NT | Dr & Mrs Good (N/S) | +1 | 430 | | 32 | 6 |
| 3NT[x] | Young Sparks 1 & 2 (N/S) | −4 | | 800 | 0 | 38 |
| 6NT[x] | Miss Judge and Miss Call (N/S) | ✓ | 1230 | | 38 | 0 |
| 3C | Others | ✓ | 110 | | 20 | 18 |
| 3C | ,, | ✓ | 110 | | 20 | 18 |
| 3C | ,, | ✓ | 110 | | 20 | 18 |
| 2NT | ,, | ✓ | 120 | | 25 | 13 |
| 2NT | ,, | ✓ | 120 | | 25 | 13 |
| 2NT | ,, | −1 | | 50 | 13 | 25 |
| 2NT | ,, | −1 | | 50 | 13 | 25 |
| 3NT | ,, | ✓ | 400 | | 28 | 10 |
| 3NT | ,, | −2 | | 100 | 7 | 31 |

Now you can see how the luck enters into duplicate. The top results on both sides were due to luck. The winning players had nothing to do with it. You play duplicate with such skill as you can assemble, but all the time Fate is hanging around, waiting to spring one of her fancy tricks.

You can't do anything about Fate.

I plead guilty to some poetic licence on this hand, but not much. Remarkable results do appear, although perhaps not all at once like this. Bridge Players are only human.

The members of The Ashen Faces, conjured out of thin air, these charming people with no existence — but they might have — are human, and therefore fallible.

So are we all. We try, my word how we try, we succeed sometimes, fail as often. At the close of day when the lights go out and Pot Luc, Miss Narrow, Joy Pretty and the rest of these insubstantial figures make their way home, that is the end of another adventure, one that was at times excruciating, at times euphoric, but uniquely worth while.

Why don't you join them?

# Information

The administration of bridge is exercised:

| | |
|---|---|
| In England | by the English Bridge Union (EBU): Broadfields, Bicester Road, Aylesbury, Bucks HP19 3BG |
| In Scotland | by the Scottish Bridge Union: 32 Whitehaugh Drive, Paisley PAI 3BG |
| In Wales | by the Welsh Bridge Union 19 Penycraig, Rhiwbina Cardiff CF4 6ST |
| In Northern Ireland | by the N.I. Bridge Union Mar Lodge, 9 Upper Malone Road, Belfast BT9 6TD |

An annual subscription is levied by these bodies, usually through the county associations. They have various functions, one of which is the Master Point scheme. You have to be a member to take part in it.

Joining is usually through your County Association – clubs carry the forms and it is automatic. Just send a cheque. Counties also run leagues, knockout events and various other competitions.

Master Points in most cases are issued by your club. You post them at intervals to headquarters, receiving in exchange a card indicating your rank. (The points the club hands out are called Local Points. 100 of these equals 1 Master Point. So the first stage, Club Master requires 200 of your points, officially 2 MP's. So multiply every number below by 100).

| Club Master | 2 MPs | | 1*Master | 100 |
|---|---|---|---|---|
| District Master | 10 | | 2* | 150 |
| County Master | 25 | | 3* | 200 |
| Master | 50 | | 4* | 250 |
| | | | 5* | 300 |

Tournament Master 400, then a * in this category for each 100 MPs.

To go any higher you will need green points, given out at special events, EBU congresses, national competitions and so on. I will not bother you with all the figures, but these are the ranks – and most also have * ranks included in them: Regional Master, Premier Regional, National, Premier National, Life, Premier Life and, top of the tree, Grand Master. Actually there is one more, proclaimed from elsewhere: World Master.

It is a long, long ladder.

Your promotions will be listed in the EBU magazine which comes to you bi-monthly without charge. The magazine, apart from its editorial content, contains many advertisements for novice and one-day events, weekend or longer bridge holidays at home and abroad and much else.

The EBU also issues a year book which includes permitted conventions, changes to the rules, reminders of procedures and other technicalities.

Other magazines are:

Bridge
from some newsagents or on subscription (£19.95 pa) from
Pergamon Bridge
Railway Road,
Sutton Coldfield
West Midlands B73 6AZ

Bridge Plus
on subscription (£14.50 pa)
from Mr Bridge Ltd.
Ryden Grange
Bisley, Surrey
GH21 2TH

Prices of these, and other items to follow, correct at autumn 1990.

## Bridge stationery

Travellers, curtain cards, Howell cards, name slips, bridge tables and cloths, playing cards and other supplies are obtainable from various sources, among them:

A. L. Fleming
8 Mason's Hill
Bromley
Kent BR2 9HA
(081 313 0350)
Price lists on request

Tatlow, White & Beard
19 Balfour Terrace
Devonport
Plymouth PL2 1RS
(0752 550838)

Individual movements require special travellers (from the above) and special table sheets directing the players to their positions. These, called Glennicks, from:

Wimbledon Bridge Enterprises
6 Walnut Tree Cottages
London SW19 5DN
(081 946 9500)

Flemings
Tatlow, White & Beard

Cost: 2 and 3 tables (8 – 15 players) £6.50; 4 and 5 tables (16 – 23 players) £6.50; 6 – 17 tables, £4.50 a table.

## Bridge books

From various suppliers as above and, of course, from bookshops. The most comprehensive source – telephone first – is: Bibliagora, 28 Pates Manor Road, Bedfont Green, Feltham, Middlesex TW14 8JF
(081 898 1234)

My own books, 'The First Bridge Book' (with the late Jeremy Flint) and 'Understanding Duplicate' from Wimbledon Bridge Enterprises (above), major bookshops, Bibliagora, Flemings, Tatlow, White & Beard.